Tim Graves
Matt 28:19

TRANSFORMED

BY THE

TRINITY

———

TONY EVANS

HARVEST HOUSE PUBLISHERS
EUGENE, OREGON

Cover by Studio Gearbox
Cover image © by Baghost / Shutterstock
Interior design by Chad Dougherty and KUHN Design Group

Select material adapted from:
The Power of God's Names © 2014 by Tony Evans
The Power of Jesus' Names © 2019 by Tony Evans
The Power of the Holy Spirit's Names © 2023 by Tony Evans

For bulk, special sales, or ministry purchases, please call 1-800-547-8979.
Email: Customerservice@hhpbooks.com

Transformed by the Trinity
Copyright © 2023 by Tony Evans
Published by Harvest House Publishers
Eugene, Oregon 97408
www.harvesthousepublishers.com

ISBN 978-0-7369-8505-5 (Milano Softone™)
ISBN 978-0-7369-8506-2 (eBook)

Library of Congress Control Number: 2023934168

Printed in China

23 24 25 26 27 28 29 30 31 / RDS / 10 9 8 7 6 5 4 3 2 1

CONTENTS

Seek His Name—
God, Jesus, Holy Spirit

Those who know Your name will put their trust in You,
for You, O LORD, have not forsaken those who seek You.

PSALM 9:10

Names matter.

When you say the name of a person, you are speaking of their identity. If you were to approach a group of people you know and ask to speak to Avery, Avery would answer. It wouldn't be Shawn. Avery would answer because that is his name. That is his identity.

Our name provides us with a way to connect with others. And when it's mentioned in conversation, it likely ushers to the hearer's mind a list of our characteristics or memories of things we've done—good or bad. It might even bring to their mind what others have said about us.

If names matter to us, you can imagine they matter all the more to God—the Creator and originator of humanity in whose image we've been made. And God's names, like ours, inform people of His characteristics, His nature, and what they can know of His faithfulness and power in individual lives and throughout history.

"I have made Your name known to them,
and will make it known."

JOHN 17:26

Once you start learning more about your God, you will be proclaiming His glory and making His names known. Exploring God's names is more than simply learning new words or discovering different titles He goes by. Pursuing God by knowing His names opens the door to knowing His character more fully and experiencing His power more deeply, personally.

Not only does God the Father go by many meaningful names, but Jesus—God the Son—has many names Himself, as does the Holy Spirit. In this book, we'll look at a selection of names for each member of the Godhead. This journey is your invitation to experience the power and life in those names.

If you've struggled in your faith walk, prayer life, or commitment to abide with God, or if you're ready to deepen your reliance on the Father, Son, and Spirit, this interactive devotional will be transformative. Not because of me and my words but because these offerings direct you to the heart and character of your God.

When we know God's character and His capacity, we find rest and discover peace and power in His covenantal care of us. Friend, God has a name for every situation we find ourselves in. Every single thing you're experiencing can lead you to a name of God, Jesus, or the Holy Spirit for guidance, hope, and strength.

———

This book's format is designed so you can engage with each presented name of God, Jesus, and the Holy Spirit through four days; spend two days experiencing, interacting, and praying with the name; and then set aside a Sabbath day to reflect on and rest in the nature of the Godhead you've encountered. Friend, let each day's reading fill you and lead you back to the heart of God. Depending on the powerful presence of the Trinity will change your perspective, realign your priorities, and transform your daily life and eternal hope in ways you can't even imagine.

GOD

O LORD, our Lord, how majestic
is Your name in all the earth.

PSALM 8:1

Hallowed Be Thy Name

The names of God convey His intrinsic majesty and glory. They are nothing short of pure majesty! Discovering and experiencing the manifestation of His names in your own life will usher you directly into the presence of our majestic God.

To know God's names is to experience His nature, and that level of intimacy is reserved for those who humbly depend on Him alone. God will not share His glory with another. And we must humble ourselves if we really want to know Him. We must realize our insignificance before we can recognize the significance that comes only through Him. We can't know His names until we forget our own. We are to hallow His name and only His name.

In fact, the Lord's Prayer begins, "Our Father who is in heaven, hallowed be Your name" (Matthew 6:9). The word *hallowed* and the word *holy* come from the same root word, which means "apart, or sanctified." In other words, we're not to mix up God's name with anyone else's name. We're not to lump Him in with others or to toss His name out lightly. God's names are hallowed. They are to be honored, respected, and treated with the reverence they deserve.

God's names are to be treated with more respect than we would show to anyone else. We are to hallow not only the verbalization of His names but also the characteristics they convey. His name carries weight. He is the one and only true God, who operates from heaven, and we must treat Him accordingly in order to fully actualize and experience the power He longs to provide.

Above and Beyond His Creation

In the beginning God [*Elohim*] created the heavens and the earth.

GENESIS 1:1

First impressions are often lasting impressions.

I want to introduce you to the very first name God reveals to us in Scripture—*Elohim*. This name is found in Genesis, the book of the beginning, and we discover it in the very first verse.

That one line at the beginning of God's Word reveals a deep character quality of God—Creator. It's God's introduction. It's the first impression of Himself that He offers to His creation. In essence, God says, "Hello, I am *Elohim*."

Why did God choose to introduce Himself to us as *Elohim*, the strong Creator God? One of the primary reasons could be that He wants us to recognize that He is transcendent—that He is distinct from His creation. God isn't amalgamated into His creation. He is not a tree, a river, or a butterfly. Rather than being a part of His creation, God is above and outside of it.

Another reason God introduces Himself to us with His name of *Elohim* is to let us know He's set apart from the constraints of time. When we read "In the beginning God created," we discern that God created the beginning. God created time. And if God created time, then He preceded time, because He couldn't have created something that already existed.

God is not limited by time but lives in eternity. He has neither a yesterday nor a tomorrow. For all the days of your life and for eternity, you are blessed to be with and loved by the eternal, Creator God.

———

God, I praise You for the greatness of Your creative ingenuity. I adore You for the fullness of Your power. Your first impression gives me a place of strength to stand all my days. Amen.

Your All-Powerful Lord

Nothing will be impossible with God.

LUKE 1:37

Before God shows us His gentleness, His fatherhood, or His grace, He introduces Himself to us as *Elohim*, the great and powerful. Right from the start He wants to establish that He is the all-knowing, all-powerful One.

The literal translation of the name *Elohim* is "strong one." In the beginning, *Elohim* (the strong one) created. In the Bible, the term *created* is used only of God, never of men. Only God, *Elohim*, makes something out of nothing.

Perhaps this is one reason God seems to become upset or annoyed when we doubt His ability. For example, when Abraham and Sarah doubted that God could create a child through them, He replied, "Is anything too difficult for the Lord?" (Genesis 18:14). Creating a child in the aged womb of a woman was nothing compared to creating the worlds out of nothing.

In a similar vein, when Mary wondered how she, a virgin, could bear a child, the angel addressed her concerns squarely in our verse today. The Strong One doesn't need raw material with which to work. All He needs is Himself, and all you need is faith in His name that He can do all that He purposes to do in your life.

Your purpose has your name on it. Your peace has your name on it. Your provision has your name on it. Your well-being has your name on it. Your rest has your name on it.

Friend, whatever situation you're facing today or whatever challenge you're trying to overcome, I encourage you to remember the name *Elohim*. Rather than trying to visualize how God might straighten out your situation, tweak your trials, or fix your failures, remember that *Elohim* can create something out of nothing.

God, forgive me when I fail to recognize Your creative power and for not pausing to be awed by and appreciative of Your creation. Guide me to my destiny for Your glory. Amen.

Right Here, Right Now

"Am I a God who is near [*Elohei Mikkarov*]," declares the LORD,
"and not a God far off [*Elohei Merachok*]? Can a man hide himself
in hiding places so I do not see him?" declares the LORD.
"Do I not fill the heavens and the earth?" declares the LORD.

JEREMIAH 23:23-24

God is everywhere-present at the same time. The theological term is *omnipresent*. In today's verses, the prophet Jeremiah offers us a glimpse into this delicate balance of God's presence. He is the God who is near and the God who fills the heaven and earth.

With all the talk about God being here, there, and everywhere, we might be tempted to think of Him as an energy source. Yet the name *Elohim* doesn't mean God is like that. The Bible would never say, "May the force be with you." In fact, in Genesis 1:3-5, we see His name *Elohim* associated with some very personal attributes: "Then God [*Elohim*] *said*, 'Let there be light'; and there was light. God *saw* that the light was good; and God *separated* the light from the darkness. God *called* the light day, and the darkness He *called* night."

God said, God saw, God separated, and God called. Each of these actions clearly reveals the personal and engaging character of God. He's not merely a spirit floating around in never-never land. He is other-dimensional—and we shouldn't lose that emphasis—but He is also intensely personal.

You and I don't live in an impersonal universe. We don't reside in a universe with no one to relate to. As *Elohim*, God interacts with His creation—He personally interacts with you right here, right now.

———

God, You created light and chose the color of the sky. You put the universe together with Your words. Thank You for putting my life together as well. Amen.

Surrender to His Restoration

"For I know the plans that I have for you," declares the LORD,
"plans for prosperity and not for disaster, to give you a future and a hope."

JEREMIAH 29:11 NASB

Whatever God is going to do for you, He has already done. Whatever God has planned for you to do, He has already planned. Whatever God has purposed for your life, He has already purposed.

Scripture says, "We are His workmanship, created in Christ Jesus for good works, which God prepared beforehand so that we would walk in them" (Ephesians 2:10).

Your job as a follower of Jesus Christ isn't to try to outwit, outplay, or outsmart God—to try to figure out your personal destiny yourself. God has already drawn the map of your life, and it's a *good* life filled with both a future and a hope. You just need to obey Him fully so you can enter the rest He has planned for you.

Friend, complete the obedience He has called you to and walk in His path even when it doesn't make any sense to you (Proverbs 3:5-6). When you do, you'll discover that the strength and power that come from an all-powerful God—*Elohim*—can do things for you that you could never have imagined. In Psalm 127:2 we read, "It is vain for you to rise up early, to retire late, to eat the bread of painful labors; for He gives to His beloved even in his sleep."

You can sleep peacefully at night because you are God's beloved—you have aligned yourself under His lordship and comprehensive rule. Even something the devil has junked up, *Elohim* can fix. Never forget that He will restore your situation and your hope.

He can handle the issues of your life, make the connections and intersections you need, and give you wisdom to make the choices that will get you closer each day to the fulfillment of His will—if you will but let Him by living a life of surrender to Him.

———

God, help me be obedient and faithful. I want to discover all You have prepared for me. When I struggle or stumble, remind me that You restore my situation and hope. Amen.

Experience *Elohim*

FOCUS SCRIPTURE

God said, "Let Us make man in Our image, according to Our likeness"…God created man in His own image, in the image of God He created him; male and female He created them (Genesis 1:26-27).

How do you view your value and life knowing you're made in the image of *Elohim,* the strong creator?

_____

_____

_____

FOR REFLECTION

Describe a time you encountered God as *Elohim.*

_____

_____

_____

Which characteristic of *Elohim* draws you closer to God? Why?

_____

_____

_____

Which message from the devotions this week did you most need—and why?

_____

_____

_____

PERSONAL PRAYER

I praise You, *Elohim*, for…

_____

_____

_____

Forgive me, *Elohim*, when I…

_____

_____

_____

I'm grateful to You, *Elohim*, for…

_____

_____

_____

Elohim, today I need Your help to…

_____

_____

_____

God identifies Himself as *Elohim* 35 times. In fact, *Elohim* is the only name used for God from Genesis 1:1 to Genesis 2:3. Other names come later in His personal revelation of His character throughout His Word, but *Elohim* is emphasized in the beginning.

Your Personal God

God said to Moses, "I AM WHO I AM. This is what you are to say to the Israelites: 'I AM has sent me to you.'" God also said to Moses, "Say to the Israelites, 'The LORD, the God of your fathers—the God of Abraham, the God of Isaac and the God of Jacob—has sent me to you.'"

EXODUS 3:14-15 NIV

When the art teacher asked a young student what he was drawing, the little boy quickly replied, "I'm drawing a picture of God."

She said, "You can't! No one knows what God looks like."

To which the boy responded, "Well, they will when I'm done."

If we asked a hundred people to draw God, we would see a hundred different versions. Scripture gives us the real picture by revealing details of His character name by name.

Moses discovers an important aspect of God's image during a time he's struggling with his purpose and hiding in the desert. He's been rejected by both the Hebrews and the Egyptians, and he's insecure, fearful. So when God shows up in the midst of a burning bush and gives Moses a vision of his destiny to lead the Hebrews out of slavery in Egypt, Moses is so intimidated that he balks at God's grand request. And in my Tony Evans's translation, he says, "Okay, God, so You want me to go down and tell Pharaoh that he's supposed to let Your people go. I get that—sure. But people are going to start asking me a lot of questions, like 'Who died and made you boss?'"

God's reply is our introduction to *Jehovah*. He tells Moses to say, "I AM has sent me to you."

Jehovah ("I Am Who I Am") is God's personal name. He is our entirely self-sufficient God who reveals Himself and His sufficiency to us, often during our struggles when we're hiding instead of walking in our purpose. *Jehovah* reminds us that He is with us, and that is enough.

You and I don't need to ask God to say who He is, because the Bible already tells us.

———

God, as I explore Your Word and Your names, You are revealing a clearer picture of who You are. I may not see Your face, but You reveal Yourself to me in deep ways. Amen.

Immutable and Unchangeable

For I, the LORD, do not change.

MALACHI 3:6

We are forever changing. For instance, we get older, and eventually our hair grays and our skin sags. But God doesn't go through that process.

Jehovah, the great I Am, is immutable—He never changes. He can never become irrelevant because He's always current. Our linear, finite minds understand only what it means to go from one year to the next and then to the next. Yet God can go from here to there and back again all at the same time. He exists as the great I Am Who I Am.

So the question arises, if God doesn't change, how can He change His mind, as He did with Jonah and Nineveh (Jonah 3:10) or Moses and the Israelites (Exodus 32:14)?

The best way I know how to explain what happens when the changeless God seems to change His mind is to look at James 1:17: "Every good thing given and every perfect gift is from above, coming down from the Father of lights, with whom there is no variation or shifting shadow."

Our sun, crafted by the creator of the lights, stays hot and radiant. Yet despite its changelessness, we experience a shifting shadow when our portion of the earth is turned from it. You and I deal with shadows in our daily lives, but God, our sun, hasn't changed—we've simply moved. When we turn toward God's character and God's way, light comes where there once was darkness.

When things aren't unfolding the way we think they should, it's important to recognize that God is who He is, not who you or I want Him to be or how we choose to define Him. He is not "I am who you say I am." He is *Jehovah, Yahweh*— I Am Who I Am. He is the unchanging, radiant Son.

———

God, the shadows have been forming and seem larger than before. May I turn my feet, heart, and life toward You so that I am in Your light. Amen.

Look Beyond the Mess

Who has made man's mouth? Or who makes him mute or deaf,
or seeing or blind? Is it not I, the LORD [*Jehovah*]?

EXODUS 4:11

G od will often allow us to be in a situation with no possible solution so we can discover that *He* is our solution. He lets us hit rock bottom so we learn that He is the Rock at the bottom.

When God introduces the name *Jehovah* (Genesis 2:4), He becomes personally involved with the well-being and purpose of His creation through His plan, will, and interaction. This is precisely what He does with Moses. God pursues the attention of Moses to explain His plan for him.

Yet God didn't reveal Himself to Moses until Moses stopped what he was doing and turned to see what was going on. Sometimes in the business of life, we fail to turn aside and notice when God is trying to get our attention. After God told Moses of His plan for him, Moses started making excuses for why he couldn't follow through. He put himself down and reminded God that he couldn't even speak well, let alone speak to a pharaoh.

To this, Jehovah reminded him that *He* created that mouth. Here is God interacting with His creation at a whole new level. He is directing, commanding, and exercising His authority over it.

Is God trying to get your attention so He can interact with you personally? Perhaps something in your life doesn't quite make sense. Are you in a situation that's a mess? Maybe it even seems like a contradiction. Whatever it is, I encourage you—based on the name of *Jehovah*, who is the self-revealing One—to not simply look *at* the bush in flames. If you do, you will miss God, who wants to talk to you through the burning bush. He wants to show you a side of Him you've never seen.

God, *help me pay attention to what You're revealing about Your nature and Your plan for me. Guide my gaze so I don't focus on my mess but instead on Your message for me. Amen.*

Ask for More

Moses said, "Please, show me Your glory!"…Then the LORD said, "Behold,
there is a place by Me, and you shall stand there on the rock; and it will
come about, while My glory is passing by, that I will put you in the cleft of the
rock and cover you with My hand until I have passed by. Then I will take My
hand away and you shall see My back, but My face shall not be seen."

EXODUS 33:18, 21-23 NASB

Do you know why so many of us don't know *Jehovah* and don't experience Him personally in our daily lives? We're too busy and too distracted to ask for more of Him.

Moses could have been satisfied with the burning bush. He could have been satisfied with the ten miraculous plagues. He could have been satisfied with the parting of the sea. Yet despite all that Moses had already experienced of God and with God, he asked for more.

Too many of us are satisfied with only an introduction. Yet from the relational attribute of God as revealed through His name *Jehovah,* we can see that He will come as intimately close to us as possible—if we ask Him as Moses did.

Moses took the time to be in the presence of *Jehovah*. He turned from the distractions and quieted the noise so that in the tent of the Lord, he could ask for more.

Many believers today say they want to know God. But when you look at their lives, you see they're only asking for more from their friends, technology, entertainment—not from God. *Jehovah* knows when we're just spouting words and when we truly intend to get to know Him. Moses had dedicated the effort before he made the request of more, so God gave him something no other human on the planet has ever experienced—the personal manifest presence of God's glory.

Friend, God wants to reveal to you things you've never dreamed of. He wants you to experience His vision and plan for you. That will come about only when you get to know Him as *Jehovah*—and you keep asking for more.

———

God, I'm clearing the static and turning my attention to You. I long to know You intimately like Moses did. Prepare my heart and mind so they're ready to receive more of You. Amen.

EXPERIENCE *Jehovah*

_____

FOCUS SCRIPTURE

Moses said to God, "Suppose I go to the Israelites and say to them, 'The God of your fathers has sent me to you,' and they ask me, 'What is his name?' Then what shall I tell them?" (Exodus 3:13 NIV).

How does knowing *Jehovah* as the personal Creator help you know how to communicate who He is to others when they ask and when you're sharing your faith?

_____

_____

_____

FOR REFLECTION

Describe a time you encountered God as *Jehovah*.

_____

_____

_____

Which characteristic of *Jehovah* draws you closer to God? Why?

_____

_____

_____

Which message from the devotions this week did you most need—and why?

_____

_____

_____

PERSONAL PRAYER

I praise You, *Jehovah*, for...

_____

_____

_____

Forgive me, *Jehovah*, when I...

_____

_____

_____

I'm grateful to You, *Jehovah*, for...

_____

_____

_____

Jehovah, today I need Your help to...

_____

_____

_____

When YHWH as *Yahweh* was translated into English, it became the name most of us today know as—*Jehovah*. So when you hear the name *Jehovah*, keep in mind that this is the Hebrew name *Yahweh*, which comes from the God-given name YHWH, meaning "I am the existing one."

He Has Your Back

The mountains melted like wax at the presence of the LORD, at the presence of the Lord [*Adonai*] of the whole earth. The heavens declare His righteousness, and all the peoples have seen His glory.

PSALM 97:5-6

Poets, philosophers, preachers, and scholars throughout the ages have waxed eloquent as they pondered and wrote about mankind's place in the universe and the realization that there is Something—Someone—greater still. Yet so often people draw the conclusion that they are the masters of their fate, an idea that flies in the face of an all-knowing, all-powerful Lord and Master.

Adonai, a plural name for God, means exactly that: master and ruler. The cultural background to the singular word *Adon* is associated with masters who owned slaves. Yet it didn't merely connote ownership but conveyed a responsibility for the care and well-being of the servants. This is why the apostles often called themselves slaves of Jesus Christ. They used this language to let everyone know they were owned by Christ.

The Bible also applies the concept of ownership to a husband and wife. In 1 Peter 3:6, Sarah called Abraham "lord." The Greek word translated in this passage is *kyrios,* which is the Greek equivalent to the Hebrew word *Adon.* In my decades of pastoring and marital counseling, I've frequently heard women express concern about this concept, just as I have counseled men who struggle to put God as Lord of their life. But I believe an authentic understanding of the full weight of the term *lord* can lead to a greater feeling of freedom, because the head of a marriage is charged with the responsibility to provide for, guide, and protect those in his care.

The great and merciful *Adonai* cares for you this way. He is your protector and provider and guide. As you experience *Adonai,* you will experience freedom knowing that He will not only lead the way but also have your back.

———

God, You are great and powerful. I ask today for a humble heart that calls out to You as Master and Lord. I want You to have the lead so I am free to rest in You. Amen.

Waiting on the Promises

O Lord GOD [*Adonai Jehovah*],
how may I know that I will possess it?

GENESIS 15:8

H as this ever happened to you? You heard God's Word, and you believed that God revealed something to you, but you didn't see it come to pass. In fact, perhaps a long time passed since you believed that God had revealed His will to you, but still nothing happened.

Abram was an elderly man when God promised that He would make him a great nation and give him an heir—a child—even in his old age. And like many of us do when we hear a promise clearly from the Lord, we act on it in faith. Abram submitted to God as master and ruler and made decisions based on the promise being fulfilled. He even picked up and moved his family to the Promised Land. But once there, he waited. And waited. He was patient, but after ten years, there was no baby.

So he approached God again and called out to *Adonai*, basically asking, "How can I be sure I'll have this?" He appeals to God's character as owner.

Yes, it would have been much easier had God brought about Isaac's conception some ten years earlier. Yet God will often delay carrying out His promises until He sees a heart of surrender to Him as absolute master. Because of Abram's faithful submission, God did fulfill that promise, and not only did Abram get a new child but he received a new name—Abraham, "father of nations."

Friend, if you're making plans based on a promise from God and find yourself waiting and waiting, be sure you've taken the most important step: surrender. *Adonai* must have the right to own you if He's going to take the responsibility to do something with you.

———

God, have I fully surrendered? Search my heart for anything I'm holding back. I want You to have all of me so I can experience all of You. Amen.

Despite Our Weaknesses

Please, Lord [*Adonai*], I have never been eloquent, neither recently nor in time past, nor since You have spoken to Your servant; for I am slow of speech and slow of tongue.

EXODUS 4:10

Surrendering our insecurities to *Adonai* is how we get out of our own way to walk in the way of the Lord. Do you remember Moses's response when God called him to speak on His behalf to Pharoah? There at that burning bush, Moses started listing his flaws, including his lack as a speaker. He was convinced he didn't possess what it took to do what God asked him to do.

I've experienced this firsthand. When I was growing up, there was a time I stuttered so badly that no one could understand me. I had a desire to speak but lacked the necessary skills. *Anthony has difficulty expressing himself orally*, one teacher wrote. Not exactly someone you would expect God to call to preach the Word to tens of thousands of people at a time.

Yet that's how God works. When we surrender to Him as Lord over our life and owner of our life, He takes the raw materials of our human existence and sprinkles His power on us, suffuses His grace over us, and infuses His Spirit into us. He makes it work despite how feeble our abilities may be.

Moses recognizes his insecurities, but he also recognizes that God is in charge. He addresses God as *Adonai*, respectfully communicating his timidity. By doing so, Moses confesses that God runs this show. He may not see how this plan is possible, but he knows enough to trust *Adonai*.

Never let your self-talk or what other people say about you limit what you do for God and His kingdom. When you submit to *Adonai*, giving Him full control to direct you according to His will, He can use you in ways that will stupefy those naysayers. He did it for Abraham. He did it for Moses. He did it for me. He's done it for many, and *Adonai* can do it for you.

God, I can let go of the negative words from others and from my own mind because I have faith in Your plans. I have faith that You will use my weaknesses for Your glory. Amen.

Who Is Your Lord?

*If you confess with your mouth Jesus as Lord, and believe in your
heart that God raised Him from the dead, you will be saved;
for with the heart a person believes, resulting in righteousness,
and with the mouth he confesses, resulting in salvation.*

ROMANS 10:9-10

If you need to see more of God's rescue and deliverance in your life, perhaps you've positioned Jesus as your Savior but not as your Lord. You're not yet His slave. Keep in mind that the job of a slave is to do whatever the master says to do. It's as straightforward as that.

Unfortunately, today Jesus has to compete with too many other masters in most of our lives. But He isn't willing to be one among many. Neither is He willing to be relegated to the level of a personal assistant. "Jesus as Lord" means He's your supreme ruler and master. He calls the shots, and you acknowledge Him in everything you do. The problem is that too many people want a savior but not a lord.

The less you are a slave to Jesus Christ, the more bound you become to illegitimate strongholds. That's why so many problems appear in life. It's actually through your surrender to *Adonai* that He gives you lasting freedom.

Now, keep in mind that you can't just say, "Lord, Lord, Lord, Lord" as if it were a magic word. Confessing *Adonai* requires actions that verify His ownership everywhere He leads and directs you. The word *confess* means to openly and publicly affirm and declare where you stand on an issue. Aligning yourself underneath Jesus Christ, the *Adonai* and *Kyrios*, includes publicly declaring and demonstrating your commitment to Him. It involves displaying your association with Him in your words and actions.

Jesus declares that your willingness to confess Him becomes the marker of your seriousness about Him. So raise the white flag of surrender to the lordship of Jesus Christ and to the fulfillment of your destiny. Only then can you truly begin to enjoy being owned by Him.

——

God, I confess Jesus as Lord and believe in my heart that You are who You say You are. I need You as Savior, and I'm grateful I can call on You in times of need. I praise You. Amen.

Experience *Adonai*

FOCUS SCRIPTURE

Why do you call Me, "Lord, Lord," and do not do what I say? (Luke 6:46).

In what areas of your life are you calling on the Lord but not surrendering to *Adonai?* How is that going for you?

_____

_____

_____

FOR REFLECTION

Describe a time you encountered God as *Adonai.*

_____

_____

_____

Which characteristic of *Adonai* draws you closer to God? Why?

_____

_____

_____

Which message from the devotions this week did you most need—and why?

_____

_____

_____

PERSONAL PRAYER

I praise You, *Adonai*, for…

_____

_____

_____

Forgive me, *Adonai*, when I…

_____

_____

_____

I'm grateful to You, *Adonai*, for…

_____

_____

_____

Adonai, today I need Your help to…

_____

_____

_____

Like *Elohim*, *Adonai* is a plural word. Whenever it's used of God, it occurs in the plural because God is a plural person. He's only one God, but He's made up of plurality—the Father, the Son, and the Holy Spirit. The name *Adonai* is found more than four hundred times in the Bible and is full of meaning. It contains the concepts of dominion, rulership, and ownership.

Knowing Him Better

God tested Abraham, and said to him..."Take now your son, your only
son, whom you love, Isaac, and go to the land of Moriah, and offer him
there as a burnt offering on one of the mountains of which I will tell you."

GENESIS 22:1-2

"Tell me about yourself." At a conference, it's natural to read a fellow participant's name tag and ask them to share more about who they are. When we want to get to know God and one of His names, we can do the same.

Sometimes when God reveals Himself to someone in the Bible, He ties the name *Jehovah* to another name that reveals something deeper about Him. I call these names compound connections. God uses them to unveil Himself personally, to give people a greater revelation of His character than even the personal name *Jehovah* connotes. God often does this when people are going through difficult situations and He wants to reveal Himself as their source of help.

Jehovah Jireh means "the Lord will provide." Today's verses provide the background for the revelation of this name. And I won't lie—it's a tough situation to take in. God is testing Abraham in the most devastating way by asking that he give Him the one thing Abraham loves the most—his son. His beloved, long-anticipated child of promise, Isaac. It is a trial of the greatest magnitude.

Trials are adverse circumstances God either introduces or allows in order to identify where we are spiritually and to prepare us for where He wants us to go. If you're breathing, you cannot escape life's trials.

Abraham's trial is a test so God can check the condition of his heart and faith. We'll learn more about who God is when He's wearing the *Jehovah Jireh* name tag. If you're in a trial, take comfort knowing that trials must first pass through God's hands before reaching us. If He approves it, He must have a divine purpose for it. And as you get to know Him better, He also provides a way through.

———

God, tell me about Yourself. I want to draw closer to You. Only You know the ways my trial will be transformed by Your hands. Amen.

When It's Time to Sacrifice

Abraham rose early in the morning and saddled his donkey, and
took two of his young men with him and Isaac his son; and he
split wood for the burnt offering, and arose and went to the
place of which God had told him. On the third day Abraham
raised his eyes and saw the place from a distance.

GENESIS 22:3-4

If you have children or grandchildren, I'm sure they've boisterously asked, "How many days until Christmas?" While counting down to this pinnacle of celebration and gifts, it can be difficult for them to focus on *the* gift of that day—Jesus.

God, like any parent, doesn't want to be loved only for His gifts. As a parent, you give to your children because you love them, not so they will love you for what you can give them. God is not a cosmic bellhop. No, God loves giving from His hand as long as He knows we're really after His heart. That's why He wanted to know if Abraham would let go of his most valued possession and simply worship Him even when it hurt.

That is exactly what Abraham planned to do. He loaded up his donkeys, and without debate or pleading for an alternative, he went where God told him to go. Where did Abraham find the faith to do so? We see one answer in Hebrews 11:19: "He considered that God is able to raise people even from the dead."

Abraham knew God's request to kill Isaac seemed ridiculous from a human perspective. Yet in his pain, he trusted that even if he followed through and sacrificed Isaac, God—who had produced life through two worn-out bodies—could no doubt resurrect Isaac from the dead. He held on to that hope in *Jehovah Jireh* even though he did not know His plan.

Have you faced great sacrifice? An unbearable letting go that pained you? View that time through the hope of this truth: Sometimes God allows you to be in a situation that only He can solve so you can recognize that He is the one who solved it.

———

God, *lately I've placed more value on things of the world than on You. Today I sacrifice those objects as an offering. And with faith I will trust Your plan for me. Amen.*

God Is Your Provision

Abraham raised his eyes and looked, and behold, behind him a ram
caught in the thicket by his horns; and Abraham went and took the
ram and offered him up for a burnt offering in the place of his son.

GENESIS 22:13

While Abraham was going up the mountain to face his trial, God had his solution (the ram) coming up the other side. But Abraham didn't hear the ram that was to be sacrificed in place of Isaac until he showed obedience to God's command. He didn't see the intended sacrifice until the angel of the Lord intervened and stopped Abraham from killing his son.

That day, Abraham discovered something lifechanging about *Jehovah*. But we can easily miss the key to Abraham's provision: He could keep going until the provision of the ram came because he was able to look spiritually at the Lord (also "raising his eyes") despite the physical trial. Jesus referred to this in John 8:56.

The root word for the name *Jireh* means "to see." When *Jehovah* and *Jireh* are put together, the compound connection means "to provide." Knowing that what he saw in the spiritual realm affected his actions in the physical realm, Abraham recognized the power of sight in calling this place *Jehovah Jireh*.

God's provision for Abraham was based on His vision of what Abraham did. So the question is, what must God see so that He might provide for you when you're caught in a trial? He needs to see the same things He saw in Abraham—immediate action and obedience. Many of us don't know God as *Jehovah Jireh* because God is still waiting for us to act on what He has said.

Whatever it is you don't want to sacrifice—career, relationships, finances, even family—you must let go in order to experience *Jehovah Jireh*. When God sees you honor Him the way Abraham did, you'll discover the power and provision of *Jehovah Jireh* in your life.

———

God, I will be quick to show my faithfulness and obedience to You even though I don't know what is to come next. Amen.

The Giver of the Blessing

Abraham called the name of that place The LORD Will Provide, as it is said to this day, "In the mount of the LORD it will be provided."

GENESIS 22:14

Growing up in urban Baltimore, Maryland, little did I know that one of the defining moments in my life would take place during an unexpected trial, on a football field called the Diamond located just a few blocks from my home.

As I ran toward the end zone with the ball, a simple cross-body block snapped my right leg in two. Even then I knew God's will and way are perfect even when He asks us for sacrifice. As I laid there waiting for the ambulance in pain, I prayed, *God, You know I love football more than anything. But I'm going to thank You in the middle of this pain and loss. I know You have a plan for my life, and I give You my life to fulfill Your plan.* Not long after that, God sealed in me a commitment to full-time ministry, and there's been no turning back.

Everyone watching the game that day saw a leg break. Yet for me, the trial unveiled the name *Jehovah Jireh* and the direction of my life. Unfortunately, we often miss the purpose of the test because we become fixated on the circumstances or the stress.

Abraham was asked to take Isaac up that mountain because God wanted to know which meant more to him—Him or Isaac, the giver of the blessing or the blessing itself. Sometimes we can fall so in love with a blessing that it trumps the One who blessed us.

Regardless of how painful it is to give up the thing you love the most, always know that God has a plan and a purpose in life's trials. Because of that, in the middle of any crisis we can thank *Jehovah Jireh* for providing the plan He has for beyond the end zone of our trial.

God, even when You call me to let go of something I love, I am grateful for Your leading. I surrender to Your provision and direction. Amen.

EXPERIENCE *Jehovah Jireh*

FOCUS SCRIPTURE

Abraham stretched out his hand and took the knife to slay his son. But the angel of the LORD called to him from heaven and said…"Do not stretch out your hand against the lad, and do nothing to him; for now I know that you fear God, since you have not withheld your son, your only son, from Me" (Genesis 22:10-12).

Describe a time when God asked you to show your faithfulness to Him by sacrificing something of importance to you. What happened?

_____

_____

_____

FOR REFLECTION

Describe a time you encountered God as *Jehovah Jireh*.

_____

_____

_____

Which characteristic of *Jehovah Jireh* draws you closer to God? Why?

_____

_____

_____

Which message from the devotions this week did you most need—and why?

_____

_____

_____

PERSONAL PRAYER

I praise You, *Jehovah Jireh*, for…

_____

_____

_____

Forgive me, *Jehovah Jireh*, when I…

_____

_____

_____

I'm grateful to You, *Jehovah Jireh*, for…

_____

_____

_____

Jehovah Jireh, today I need Your help to…

_____

_____

_____

When we look at another form of the word *provide—provision*—we see this link between seeing and providing. To have vision is to see. Provision means something was seen beforehand and thus provided for. The root *vision* ties the provision to what was seen.

Anticipating Giants

There was war at Gath again, where there was a man of great
stature who had six fingers on each hand and six toes on each foot,
twenty-four in number; and he also had been born to the giant.

2 SAMUEL 21:20

One Sunday I uncharacteristically decided to continue speaking on the topic of the previous week rather than start my new sermon series. In this sequel sermon about fears and obstacles, I said, "Getting on an airplane could be a giant in your life, because you shake at the fear of flying."

The next day was my birthday, and it was filled with family and joy. But the day after that, our nation experienced one of the worst tragedies in its history. Two airplanes were deliberately crashed into the Twin Towers in New York City. One plane went down in a field in Pennsylvania. And another plane flew into the Pentagon in Virginia near Washington, D.C.

Later, after processing the shock, it struck me as odd that I used the example of getting on a plane since that's not a fear in my life. In hindsight, I could see that while I was merely talking about a fear of flying, God was highlighting the danger of much scarier giants.

America is still courageously rebuilding and restoring since that tragic day. Yet many of us have a lingering tendency to look over our shoulder or think twice about booking a flight. A giant isn't easy to forget or take down.

Most of us can handle life's normal challenges. They annoy us, but when they appear, we manage to keep going. Yet when that one *giant* shows up, that changes everything. David of the Bible found this out. Next, we'll look at his famous battle with Goliath, an actual giant and foe. And we'll pay close attention to the power of *Jehovah Tsaba*, the Lord Our Warrior, who didn't allow David to fall but instead filled him with courage and strength. No matter what you face today, you can fall to your knees and pray to *Jehovah Tsaba* to bring your giant to *its* knees.

———

God, I know giants are up ahead along my life path, but You will be there battling my foes every step of the way. I release my worry and embrace my trust and faith in You. Amen.

The Challenge Is On

Why do you come out to draw up in battle array? Am I not the Philistine and you servants of Saul? Choose a man for yourselves and let him come down to me. If he is able to fight with me and kill me, then we will become your servants; but if I prevail against him and kill him, then you shall become our servants and serve us.

1 SAMUEL 17:8-9

Today's verses are basically a throw-down challenge from the Philistines to the Israelites. They boldly call out for a representation battle where a single warrior from each side will fight until one is victorious on behalf of their group. They're confident because Goliath, a giant of mammoth proportions, is their representative. His 40 days of taunts leave the Israelites so fearful that the king promises great riches and his daughter to whoever can bring down Goliath.

Enter David. His father sent him to the front lines with food for his brothers. Once there, David, who was small in stature compared to the Philistine, looked straight ahead at Goliath's midsection. From this vantage point, he zeroed in on a critical reality: *Goliath had not been circumcised.*

David said, "What will be done for the man who kills this Philistine and takes away the reproach from Israel? For who is this *uncircumcised* Philistine, that he should taunt the armies of the living God?" (1 Samuel 17:26). Uncircumcised meant that Goliath was not in the family of God and would have no divine covering.

David's perspective wasn't like everyone else's. The Israelites looked up at Goliath's size, strength, and armor. But David looked straight ahead and saw proof that this giant was no competition for *Jehovah Tsaba*. I imagine David pointing and saying, "I've got it because God's got it. That man has not been cut."

Perspective is never just what you see; it's how you *view* what you see. Take a second to look at your particular giant. It is beatable, my friend—not because of your might but because your giant is no match for God. It's a game changer when *Jehovah Tsaba* is your representative in your righteous battle.

God, *anything that causes fear within me is insignificant when in Your presence. I can stand strong today because You stand strong on my behalf for eternity. Amen.*

Choose Your Weapon

You come to me with a sword, a spear, and a javelin, but I come to you in the name of the LORD of hosts [*Jehovah Tsaba*], the God of the armies of Israel, whom you have taunted. This day the LORD will deliver you up into my hands, and I will strike you down and remove your head from you.

1 SAMUEL 17:45-46

Sometimes God allows you to experience a bigger-than-life Goliath so you'll experience a bigger-than-Goliath God. David knew this before anyone twice his age or twice his size did because he saw what the others couldn't: the spiritual reality. They saw only the physical problem, which is why Saul summons David to basically say, "Thanks, but no thanks. You're no match for this giant."

David tells them all he has killed a lion and a bear, then adds, "This *uncircumcised* Philistine will be like one of them, since he has taunted the armies of the living God" (1 Samuel 17:36). Saul acquiesces and loads David with armor so heavy that the boy can barely walk.

At this point, young David made a manly decision—he took off the physical armor and chose to fight the giant in his own anointing and with the tools he had. He didn't choose armor or weapons designed for the physical battle his fellow Israelites predicted; he chose weapons suited to the *spiritual battle* God planned for His victory. Along with his faith, David had five smooth stones from the brook, a sling, and his secret weapon—*Jehovah Tsaba*.

David ignores Goliath's disdain and mocking and gives the epic speech we read in today's verses. He's confident for battle because he's armed with all he needs.

Giants rule many of our hearts and our homes today because we've lost the ability to see the important spiritual battles behind the obvious physical ones. And because of that, we don't choose the right weapons to take down our personal Goliaths. My friend, God has a unique way He wants to take you to your destination. And unlike Saul's attempt to arm David with what he didn't need, God arms you with exactly what you need: the power of His names.

———

God, when I'm restless with concerns and questions, I can come to You, my bigger-than-Goliath God. My faith is fortified when I face struggles in Your name. Amen.

The Battle Belongs to God

David put his hand into his bag and took from it a stone and slung it, and struck the Philistine on his forehead...Thus David prevailed over the Philistine with a sling and a stone, and he struck the Philistine and killed him; but there was no sword in David's hand.

1 SAMUEL 17:49-50

Friend, the names of God are powerful and uniquely crafted to your situations. And He has issued you the authority to use them in line with His will.

By advancing in God's name, David positioned himself to defeat someone seemingly undefeatable. He gave the battle over to God. That doesn't mean he sat and did nothing. He did all he could, but he did it with one truth in mind—God would give Goliath into his hands. Not because Goliath was taunting David but because Goliath was taunting God and His people. That doesn't sit too well with the King.

Like the Israelites, many of us are so busy trying to figure out how we're supposed to conquer our giants that we don't ask the most important question: *What does God say about this?*

When you're wondering how to overcome your opposition—including internal opposition, such as addiction, fear, or low self-esteem—you're thinking the battle is yours. And in that case, you're not likely to succeed, for "our struggle is not against flesh and blood, but against the rulers, against the powers, against the world forces of this darkness, against the spiritual forces of wickedness in the heavenly places" (Ephesians 6:12). And no offense, but you're not smart enough or strong enough to beat an enemy from another realm. The battle belongs to *Jehovah Tsaba*.

Some of the most incredible things God will ever do in your life will occur when you think you're not positioned to move forward, make that change, advance in your destiny, defeat your giant. But that's precisely when God shows up. When He wins your battle, you know who did it. You know who ought to get the glory. And when the next giant shows up, you know who will defeat him too—*Jehovah Tsaba*.

———

God, *I want to know what You think about my current circumstance. You create the master strategy for my life, and I'm ready and eager to move forward in it. Amen.*

EXPERIENCE *Jehovah Tsaba*

_____

FOCUS SCRIPTURE

When the Philistine looked and saw David, he disdained him; for he was but a youth, and ruddy, with a handsome appearance. The Philistine said to David, "Am I a dog, that you come to me with sticks?" And the Philistine cursed David by his gods (1 Samuel 17:42-43).

When have your faith and your strength in God been underestimated by someone? How did you respond?

_____

_____

_____

FOR REFLECTION

Describe a time you encountered God as *Jehovah Tsaba*.

_____

_____

_____

Which characteristic of *Jehovah Tsaba* draws you closer to God? Why?

_____

_____

_____

Which message from the devotions this week did you most need—and why?

_____

_____

_____

PERSONAL PRAYER

I praise You, *Jehovah Tsaba*, for…

_____

_____

_____

Forgive me, *Jehovah Tsaba*, when I…

_____

_____

_____

I'm grateful to You, *Jehovah Tsaba*, for…

_____

_____

_____

Jehovah Tsaba, today I need Your help to…

_____

_____

_____

The name *Tsaba* essentially means "army, or host." David knew that because God was the Lord of the army and the creator over all, the victory was His.

Too Much Drama

The LORD will give strength to His people;
The LORD will bless His people with peace.

PSALM 29:11

Turmoil. It's a word that accurately describes our present day. Tragic occurrences are everywhere. Mass shootings, terrorism, war, crime. Closer to home, we often see conflict in our own churches through socioeconomic, denominational, or racial divides.

There's also turmoil in our homes as evidenced by the divorce rate. Many couples today seem to be married by the secretary of defense rather than the justice of the peace, creating a battleground where arguments, misunderstandings, neglect, and even physical and emotional abuse take place.

Yet the worst turmoil of all often takes place in one's own soul. This happens when you can't seem to live with yourself, when your own pain, anxiety, depression, and regret eat you up, leaving you with an unsettled ache. You are at war within.

These days, some trade the word *turmoil* for the word *drama*. And do we ever live lives full of unending drama—our own or other people's. We don't desire this drama, but once it's here, we're not quite sure how to get rid of it. Things seem to have gotten so bad for so many that clinical depression and other emotional disorders are on the rise as people search for escape—some way to numb the pain, remove the anguish, and discover some momentary peace.

Even though we experience turmoil on so many levels in our contemporary world, turmoil itself is nothing new. The search for peace and tranquility spans ages and cultures. But we, my friend, know where to go. We know the source of a peace that goes beyond our human comprehension of a mere calmness. Let us pursue Him as "the Lord is peace." Let us ditch the drama and rejoice in the stability and security of *Jehovah Shalom*—the One who brings peace no matter the storm.

———

God, turmoil takes up too much of my time and energy. I choose Your peace. May it change my thoughts and emotions. I don't want to be drawn to drama—ever. Amen.

Rock Bottom

Israel was brought very low because of Midian,
and the sons of Israel cried out to the LORD.

JUDGES 6:6

When we're caught in the drama, we love to believe peace will come as soon as we get to the corner office, the larger house, that destination wedding in Belize. But in truth, if you've taken your eyes off God, you can even be in the promised land, the destination God has for you, and be light-years from His peace and destiny.

That was the chaotic situation in which the Israelites found themselves. God had sent them into the Promised Land to have victory over their enemies. But because of their disobedience and rebellion, He allowed their enemies, the Midianites, to defeat them so often that the Israelites were now hungry, broken, and in hiding.

God let them hit rock bottom, just as He sometimes lets us hit rock bottom when we've walked away from Him in our hearts and actions. He lets us go so low that we'll realize He's our only way back up.

Finally, after years of worshiping idols and turning away from the true God, the Israelites cried out in desperation. Often, people finally cry out to God when they're so deep in turmoil that they have nowhere else to turn. Their prayers are no longer cute religious recitations; they're raw "life just got real" ugly cries. And God, who has every right to ignore the pleas of sinners, recognizes the possibility of these moments. He knows He has their ear, their attention, and their readiness for surrender. Are you at that point of surrender?

As God did for the Israelites, He will hear your cries. He will remind you that He is the one who saved, delivered, and protected you before, but He graciously receives you in the middle of the mess you may very well have caused, and He shares His plan for your ultimate peace.

———

God, in my brokenness, I admit that I'm not in control—and I never was. Why has it taken me so long to surrender? I give to You my all. Amen.

Peace in Your Presence

The angel of the LORD vanished from his sight. When Gideon saw that
he was the angel of the LORD, he said, "Alas, O Lord GOD! For now I
have seen the angel of the LORD face to face." The LORD said to him,
"Peace to you, do not fear; you shall not die." Then Gideon built an altar
there to the LORD and named it The LORD is Peace [*Jehovah Shalom*].

JUDGES 6:21-24

Without God's presence, you can go and do whatever you want, but you won't
have peace. God knows this. So when the Israelites cried out to Him, the
Lord made His presence known by sending an angel to a young man named Gideon.
The angel told him, "The LORD is with you, O valiant warrior" (Judges 6:12).

The angel of the Lord addressed Gideon as a valiant warrior. Yet Gideon had
fought no battles and won no wars. He was simply trying to survive. Gideon basically responds, "Hey, if God is for me, then where is He? If He can do miracles,
why is life a mess?"

It wasn't enough to hear of a big plan and God's belief in him—Gideon needed
God.

And God needed Gideon. He planned to deliver the Israelites from the Midianites through this young man. Instead of choosing a leader or doing it on His
own, God chose this guy hiding out in a winepress. A lot like Moses did, Gideon
responded to God's calling with a list of the reasons he thought he *wasn't* the wis-
est, most capable choice. Gideon was fearful and desperately needed to know that
God was right there with him. He asked for a sign. The angel of the Lord sent fire
from a rock to consume the meat and unleavened bread Gideon had served Him.

That was when Gideon built an altar and named it "The LORD is Peace." Not
because the battle and the turmoil were over, but because God was there. Friend,
in your drama or struggle, don't look to the victory to experience the peace; look
to *Jehovah Shalom* and experience the peace of His presence.

———

*God, I feel Your peace even as the battle rages on. When I place my faith in Your presence,
the chaos is muted. You are the one I hear, and my heart is relieved. Amen.*

Set Your Mind on Him

*You will keep in perfect peace those whose minds are steadfast,
because they trust in you.*

ISAIAH 26:3 NIV

Friend, do you want peace? Only one person can give it—*Jehovah Shalom*. But He gives it only on His terms. In order to transform what you do, you must first transform what you think. For Gideon, that meant knowing God was not only with him but also for him.

The mind set on the Spirit—that which seeks to align your thoughts underneath God's point of view—is the mind full of peace. As Paul states in his letter to the church at Rome, "The mind set on the flesh is death, but the mind set on the Spirit is life and peace" (Romans 8:6).

A mind set on God's presence, just as Gideon's was, brings life and peace—*shalom*. But the mind set on the flesh is set on death and separation from God, and it never brings peace.

When you continue to set your mind on the Spirit, you develop a habit of abiding in Him. If you're not used to hanging out with God—setting your mind on the Spirit—you need to proactively seek Him, His Word, and His ways in order to abide in His peace. Yet in time, this will become more natural and personal, and relational peace will become a way of life rather than a place you visit from time to time.

Before the conductor of an orchestra walks onto the stage, the sounds coming from the instruments are in discord. But when he arrives, the chaos is stilled. He raises his baton, and the musicians' submission to his direction results in beautiful harmony. God is your maestro. Seek His presence, place your trust in Him, submit to His leading, and make a soundtrack of peace with *Jehovah Shalom*.

———

God, the storms come to a halt when You are near. As I pray with a surrendered heart, I feel and know You as my shelter, my hope, and my peace. Amen.

EXPERIENCE *Jehovah Shalom*

FOCUS SCRIPTURE

If only you had paid attention to my commands, your peace would have been like a river, your well-being like the waves of the sea (Isaiah 48:18 NIV).

Can you look back on your life and describe a situation where your obedience to God ushered you to waves of well-being?

_____

_____

_____

FOR REFLECTION

Describe a time you encountered God as *Jehovah Shalom*.

_____

_____

_____

Which characteristic of *Jehovah Shalom* draws you closer to God? Why?

_____

_____

_____

Which message from the devotions this week did you most need—and why?

_____

_____

_____

PERSONAL PRAYER

I praise You, *Jehovah Shalom*, for…

_____

_____

_____

Forgive me, *Jehovah Shalom,* when I…

_____

_____

_____

I'm grateful to You, *Jehovah Shalom*, for…

_____

_____

_____

Jehovah Shalom, today I need Your help to…

_____

_____

_____

Peace is bigger than calm. The word *shalom* means "wholeness, completeness, or well-being." It means having things properly aligned and ordered. It means harmony and balance. It means more than just feeling good at a particular moment. It even means more than happiness. Peace has to do with well-being regardless of circumstances. A person who is at peace is stable, calm, orderly, and at rest within.

The Big S

The LORD is my shepherd [*Jehovah Rohi*], I shall not want.

PSALM 23:1 NKJV

I love the heroic character Superman. In one movie featuring him, a man was trapped in an inferno and Superman swooped in and rescued him from certain death. Later, as Superman was flying across the sky to take the man home, the trembling guy said, "I'm afraid…way up here, and if I fall, I'm going to die."

Superman responds, "Do you think I have enough power to save you from the fire but not enough power to safely take you home?"

This illustration hits close to home for some of us who limit our trust in the Lord. We trust Him to deliver us from the fires of hell, yet we're not sure He can safely take us home or care for our needs. If you're one of these people, this next name of God is just for you: *Jehovah Rohi*, or Shepherd.

God expects a shepherd to feed the flock, strengthen the weak, heal the sick, bind up the broken, bring back the strays, and seek the lost (Ezekiel 34:2-4). *Jehovah Rohi* has got you covered. But in order for Him to be your Shepherd, you must first recognize yourself as a sheep. Full disclosure: Sheep are known to be defenseless, dirty, dependent, and…dumb. They have to be fed and led by a shepherd to survive. David says his Shepherd, the Lord, has the power to meet all of these needs.

The same is true for you, my friend. In fact, the Good Shepherd, *Jehovah Rohi*, not only tends to our needs but is willing to lay down His life for us, His sheep (John 10:11). So when you feel sheepish and scared and look to the sky for the "big S" hero, forgo the one in the cape and run to the One on the cross. Only He is your Savior and Shepherd.

———

God, *because of You, goodness and mercy will follow me all the days of my life. I long to dwell in Your house, and I'm so grateful that You lead me there safely. Amen.*

Rest in Him

He makes me to lie down in green pastures; He leads
me beside the still waters. He restores my soul.

PSALM 23:2-3 NKJV

Has your spiritual get-up-and-go gotten up and gone?
Maybe right now God seems to be a long way away. Or daily life is beating you down. But despite the dearth, you still feel an ache inside reminding you that you want to be restored. You just don't know how.

David explains how *Jehovah Rohi* restores your soul. First, He makes you to lie down in green pastures. Notice He doesn't *suggest* you lie down—remember, we're talking about sheep here. He *makes* you lie down. Have you considered that perhaps God hasn't changed the situation you're in because He's waiting for you to relinquish your rebellion and self-sufficiency and depend on Him?

Maybe this will nudge you to take a needed break: When you do lie down, you'll discover what David discovered—that God chooses the greenest of pastures. He gives you the softest mattress and the fluffiest pillow because He longs to see you recover. He also leads you to still waters. A good shepherd doesn't let sheep drink from rushing waters, because they're not sure-footed. He keeps them safe so they can be refreshed.

When we rest in *Jehovah Rohi*, He leads us into safe environments. But we won't discover the blessing of rest and still waters as long as we remain self-sufficient and think we can fix our problems, including our soul weariness.

If we stall or rebel before we're willing to lie down, God continues to allow scenarios that force us to rest, let go, and trust Him to care for us. And when we do let go, we discover—just as David wrote—that God will restore our soul. It takes time, but the result is worth it. As we rest in Him, He restores our sense of hope, purpose, and life.

———

God, You call me to take a rest, to drink from the stream of refreshment, and to follow You close. Thank You for Your gentleness and kindness. Amen.

Before the Mountain

He leads me in the paths of righteousness for His name's sake. Yea,
though I walk through the valley of the shadow of death, I will fear no
evil; for You *are* with me; Your rod and Your staff, they comfort me.

PSALM 23:3-4 NKJV

When we look back over our lives, we remember making some wrong turns, unwise decisions, or ill-advised choices. If given the chance to live those years over again, would we make the same miscalculations and mistakes? Probably not. In hindsight, we can see our paths to righteousness and abundant life more clearly. Yet God, your Shepherd, wants to direct you on the right path in each and every decision—if you will but seek and follow Him.

Not only that, but God can get you back on the right path if you've wandered away and ended up in a valley, a place of vulnerability and risk. A valley at night can be frightening for sheep. They would be easy prey for the animals that come out when darkness falls if not for their faithful shepherd who walks with them in those shadows.

Everyone loves the view from the top of a mountain. When your job, health, family, finances, and faith are good, you can feel on top of the world. You can't leap from mountaintop to mountaintop, however; you have to go through the valley between. But the good thing about a valley is that it reminds us that another mountain is up ahead.

When you're in the valley of the shadows and you just want to give up and quit, *Jehovah Rohi* is there with you. That doesn't mean you won't feel afraid. David didn't deny the reality of the shadow of death. He affirmed that despite how everything looks in the valley, we're not to give in to fear because the presence of God, His rod, and His staff comfort us. We are not alone.

No matter what you face today, know that you're safer in a dark valley in the presence of God than you would be anywhere else without Him.

———

God, whenever I'm back in the valley, my heart still praises You. You are my comfort, and You lead me step by step to the next mountain. Thank You, Lord. Amen.

Protected and Anointed

You prepare a table before me in the presence of my enemies;
You anoint my head with oil; my cup runs over.

PSALM 23:5 NKJV

An enemy is any threat to your security. It can show up in a person, in a thing, and most certainly in the devil himself. Yet David assures us that God prepares a table before us in plain view of those who are against us. Now, if the thought of dining on a pot roast while our enemies watch kills our appetites, that's because we're focusing on the food and the enemies, not on our host, *Jehovah Rohi*.

In Bible times, a shepherd carried a belt that held a cloth. Whenever he found a lost sheep, he spread out the cloth and set some grass and fodder on it so the lost sheep could eat. While the sheep was eating under the protective eye of the shepherd, the foxes and coyotes kept their distance.

Fundamental to our understanding of God as our Shepherd is the realization that the Lord Himself is the one who prepares our table. In His presence, we are safe from our enemies. God is bigger than all of them. He knows how to provide for us in a bad situation.

Our Shepherd not only prepares a table for us in the presence of enemies but also anoints our head with oil. Sheep often wandered into thickets to search for berries. When the shepherd retrieved them, he would place oil on their heads to heal their cuts from the thorns.

Despite the presence of enemies and the wounds of life, *Jehovah Rohi* is more than enough to get you through any situation. Friend, if you look to God, you will discover that He has more than enough grace to meet your every need. Whether He administers a solution to your problem or gives you the peace necessary to sustain you while you're in the problem, His grace overflows.

———

God, I've been too focused on my enemies. Today I turn my eyes to You and trust Your protection and plan. This shift is life-giving. Amen.

EXPERIENCE *Jehovah Rohi*

FOCUS SCRIPTURE

"I will also raise up shepherds over them and they will tend them; and they will not be afraid any longer, nor be terrified, nor will any be missing," declares the LORD (Jeremiah 23:4).

Is it difficult for you to view yourself as a simple sheep under the Shepherd's care? Why or why not?

_____

_____

_____

FOR REFLECTION

Describe a time you encountered God as *Jehovah Rohi*.

_____

_____

_____

Which characteristic of *Jehovah Rohi* draws you closer to God? Why?

_____

_____

_____

Which message from the devotions this week did you most need—and why?

_____

_____

_____

PERSONAL PRAYER

I praise You, *Jehovah Rohi*, for…

_____

_____

_____

Forgive me, *Jehovah Rohi*, when I…

_____

_____

_____

I'm grateful to You, *Jehovah Rohi*, for…

_____

_____

_____

Jehovah Rohi, today I need Your help to…

_____

_____

_____

The name of God translated "LORD" in this verse is *Jehovah*, "the self-revealing one." The Hebrew word for "shepherd" is the word *rohi* or *ra'ah*, which means "to tend, pasture, shepherd." It was written by King David, who was a shepherd as a young boy.

The Lord Is My Banner

The LORD said to Moses, "Write this in a book as a memorial and recite it to Joshua, that I will utterly blot out the memory of Amalek from under heaven." Moses built an altar and named it The LORD is My Banner [*Jehovah Nissi*].

EXODUS 17:14-15

The bad news is that life has problems. The good news is that when people find themselves in difficulties that require divine intervention, God reveals Himself through a name that speaks directly to meeting the need of that moment. The LORD Is My Banner isn't as obvious as some other names, so before we look at how and why God revealed Himself in this way, let's look at what banners represent in our time.

Raised banners are often a visual declaration of commitment and allegiance. They proclaim Jesus as Lord in churches. They represent nations at the Olympic Games. And when I served as chaplain to the Dallas Mavericks and they had claimed an NBA title, their banner raised above a sold-out crowd was a celebration of victory.

In Exodus, we come across God's people when they're not celebrating their circumstances. They are in Rephidim, a desolate and dry place. Earlier they lacked water. God knew their need, saw their need, and took care of it. That provision of water refreshed them physically and most likely, for a short time, spiritually. But now, in their weariness, they're facing a determined enemy—the Amaleks—and are again wondering if God is on their side. It can be easy to judge the Israelites and their ongoing doubts, but how many of us have wondered at some point whether God is with us and for us?

Maybe this is you right now. For today, hold on to the truth that God knows and sees your need and that He will reveal Himself as the One to meet that need. In fact, maybe He's already providing for you, but you haven't yet accepted His healing or help. Watch for *Jehovah Nissi* as this story and your own story unfold under the glory of God.

God, *because of Your power to overcome, You are my banner when I need You the most. I praise You, Lord, and I seek Your covering in the trials and in the journey. Amen.*

Partner with God

Moses said to Joshua, "Choose men for us and go out, fight against Amalek. Tomorrow I will station myself on the top of the hill with the staff of God in my hand." Joshua did as Moses told him, and fought against Amalek...So it came about when Moses held his hand up, that Israel prevailed, and when he let his hand down, Amalek prevailed.

EXODUS 17:9-11

When people fight for something valuable to them—their marriage, family, health, work, destiny—some fight from the mountain only. They say, "I'm just going to trust God and talk to Him, and He will fix everything." Others seek to win the battle in the valley with only their skills, determination, and resources. But to win the battles in our lives, there must always be a balance between what God does on the mountain and what we are responsible for in the valley.

In the Bible story of the battle between the Israelites and Amalek, Amalek represents the forces of evil. Moses knew that only in his connection to God could he fight the spiritual battle and win. So he stood above it all with the staff of God in his hand. This staff was a simple shepherd's crook, but it was sanctified and significant. It was the same staff that opened up the Red Sea. Through it, God used the natural to perform the supernatural several times.

In today's verses we read that God allowed the Israelites to prevail in the battle against Amalek as long as Moses *continued* to hold up the staff. The winners and losers weren't determined by their skill; rather, the key was Moses's posture with the staff of God. The victory also required Joshua and the Israelites to do their part in the valley.

If your personal Amalek keeps prevailing, consider whether you're operating as though your actions alone will determine the outcome. Or maybe you keep looking to the mountain and waiting on God, when all the while He's waiting on your obedience in the valley. As Paul writes, "We then, as workers together *with* him" (2 Corinthians 6:1 NKJV). Friend, in your fight for what matters, join forces with *Jehovah Nissi*.

———

God, *help me release my belief that victory or change will happen in my strength! Your strength alone guides and determines the outcome of my battles as well as my growth. Amen.*

We Need Propping Up

Moses' hands were heavy. Then they took a stone and put it
under him, and he sat on it; and Aaron and Hur supported
his hands, one on one side and one on the other. Thus his
hands were steady until the sun set. So Joshua overwhelmed
Amalek and his people with the edge of the sword.

EXODUS 17:12-13

Spiritual battles can be tiresome. "Moses' hands were heavy" as he held the staff high on the hill. His staff didn't weigh any more than before, but his arms were growing weak because the battle was going long and he was growing weary.

Perhaps this has happened to you. As a trial goes on, you begin to lose interest in reading your Bible, and lifting up yet another prayer seems too hard. Your faith grows weak because your battle is going long, and you're growing weary.

The problem for the Israelites was that as Moses became tired and his arms drifted down, Amalek prevailed. So Aaron and Hur came up with a plan to maintain the spiritual power by lifting up Moses's tired arms.

The beauty of God's church is that it provides us with a place to find our own Aarons and Hurs to lift up our weary arms. It also provides us with opportunities to do that for another. One afternoon, a man in our church came to my house. He looked distraught and defeated as he described the challenges life kept throwing his way. I didn't solve his problems for him, but I reminded him of the spiritual reality behind those physical problems. I reminded him of God's victory, His power, and His presence. When it was time to go, the man was smiling, his head held high.

Even the strongest people will have times when they need propping up to keep their spirit focused Godward so they can prevail in the valleys of life. Don't throw in the towel when you've never raised the staff. Don't quit the battle when you've never raised the bar. Joshua fought in the valley and Moses on the hill. As a result, they prevailed over their enemies, just as you can prevail over yours.

God, *my arms are so tired. Whom do You have to come alongside me in this current trial? I will watch for Your help and support. I know it is right here. Amen.*

Jesus Is Our Banner

As Moses lifted up the serpent in the wilderness, even so must the Son
of Man be lifted up; so that whoever believes will in Him have eternal life.

JOHN 3:14-15

After the victory against the Amaleks, Moses built an altar and gave it the name
we've learned about here—*Jehovah Nissi*—The LORD Is My Banner. The banner was Moses's staff of God. Most of us don't have a staff of God. Yet God has
given us a banner to deal with the challenges of life in our day.

In Numbers 21, we read a story that foreshadows the banner of Christ. The people had rebelled against God, so He sent poisonous snakes that bit them. Many
of the Israelites died. It didn't matter where they went for help because theirs was
a spiritual problem.

They cried out to God, and in response He instructed Moses to put a bronze
snake on a stick and hold it up high. He told Moses to let the people of Israel know
that whoever looked at the snake on the stick (the banner lifted up) would live. But
everyone who looked to their own cure died because God had lifted up just one
banner, and only those who looked to it lived.

Friend, our *Nissi* today is Jesus Christ.

Whoever looks to Jesus, our banner, will live. Even if you're doing everything
you believe you're supposed to do, unless you're pointed toward Jesus Christ and
operate under His will, His Word, and His standard, you won't have the spiritual
help you need to deal with the battles you face in the valley.

The solution to many of your Amalek problems is right in front of you. Yet God
won't solve your problem until you look to Him as your banner. Your hands will
get heavy, and the devil will make you weary, but before you give up, look up. Fix
your eyes on Jesus, your *Nissi*. Your victory has already been won.

God, *keep me pointed toward You. I have fallen prey to all the distractions lately. You are my
banner, my Savior. I will fix my eyes on You. Amen.*

EXPERIENCE *Jehovah Nissi*

FOCUS SCRIPTURE

You have given a banner to those who fear You, that it may be displayed because of the truth (Psalm 60:4).

How have you displayed your banner of belief for the world to see? How do you proclaim God's truth?

_____

_____

_____

FOR REFLECTION

Describe a time you encountered God as *Jehovah Nissi.*

_____

_____

_____

Which characteristic of *Jehovah Nissi* draws you closer to God? Why?

_____

_____

_____

Which message from the devotions this week did you most need—and why?

_____

_____

_____

PERSONAL PRAYER

I praise You, *Jehovah Nissi*, for…

_____

_____

_____

Forgive me, *Jehovah Nissi*, when I…

_____

_____

_____

I'm grateful to You, *Jehovah Nissi*, for…

_____

_____

_____

Jehovah Nissi, today I need Your help to…

_____

_____

_____

For many of us, holding up a banner is akin to holding up a flag or piece of cloth or material. But in biblical times, a banner could refer to any number of items, including those explored here—the staff and the bronze serpent on a pole.

Life-Giving

God blessed the seventh day and sanctified it,
because in it He rested from all His work
which God had created and made.

GENESIS 2:3

W hen did you last use the word *sanctify* in conversation? Even the most faithful would be scratching their heads trying to recall a time, let alone during a casual chat with a friend. Our next name of God means "the Lord who sanctifies." But before we look at where this name first appears, I want to pause so we can grasp what "to sanctify" means. To understand it, we can first look at three words—*common*, *profane*, and *sacred*.

That which is common, God has created as ordinary. It exists for the general welfare and the good of those involved. That which is profane includes those things that are polluted, defiled, or contaminated. These are destructive actions, attitudes, and people. That which is sacred is special to God and reflects His glory. These unique things include God's presence, sanctions, and purposes.

Something becomes sanctified when it's set apart from the common, ordinary, and regular things of life. It's made to be special, unique, one of a kind, holy. It transfers from the realm of the common into the realm of the sacred.

When God created the days of the week, He declared each day to be good. Today's Scripture tells us that when He arrived at the seventh day (Saturday), He rested and sanctified that day as holy. Sanctifying the seventh day didn't make the other six days bad; it just meant they weren't sanctified, holy. In fact, God instructed His people to remember the Sabbath day to keep it holy.

As we'll discover, people can be sanctified too.

Jehovah Mekoddishkem is a life-giving name. Nestled in Leviticus, the "book of life" itself is the secret to experiencing all the life God has for us to experience. And, friend, that's a secret you don't want to miss.

God, *because of You, I am not common or profane. I praise Your name, for You have set me apart and made me holy so that I might reflect Your glory. Amen.*

Holy for God

You shall consecrate yourselves therefore and be holy, for I
am the LORD your God. You shall keep My statutes and
practice them; I am the LORD who sanctifies you.

LEVITICUS 20:7-8

The name *Jehovah Mekoddishkem* is a little different from the other names we're studying. This name of God infuses power into our lives when we receive by faith everything He seeks to do in and through us.

But how do you and I become sanctified? Sanctification signifies an action done to us. It's the process of God setting us apart *from* sin and unrighteousness and *to* His person and purposes. He makes us unique, set apart, and holy to live under God and His comprehensive rule according to His kingdom agenda.

Throughout Leviticus, God is getting His children ready for their destiny by instructing them how to worship and walk with Him once they get there. God knows their success in the Promised Land will depend on their relationship with Him. He wants the best for them, so He explains His expectations and the key to His provisions in this new chapter of their lives.

In today's passage, only one of two where the Hebrew references *Jehovah Mekoddishkem,* God reminds the Israelites that He is the God who brought them out of slavery, out of Egypt, and that He did this for a purpose—to be *Jehovah Mekoddishkem* to them. To sanctify them. He did this then just as now He seeks to sanctify you and me through the death, burial, and resurrection of Jesus Christ.

God was preparing the Israelites for their destiny and for a life of being "set apart" for Him, and He prepares us and sanctifies us for our purpose and destiny in Him. He calls us to follow His statutes and abide in Him as His holy people and to receive by faith everything He wants to do in and through us.

———

God, I'm excited about what You have in store for me. Thank You for preparing my path and my heart so I'll be worthy and able to walk in Your purpose. Amen.

Set Apart for His Purpose

I have said to you, "You are to possess their land, and I Myself will give it to you to possess it, a land flowing with milk and honey." I am the LORD your God, who has separated you from the peoples...Thus you are to be holy to Me, for I the LORD am holy; and I have set you apart from the peoples to be Mine.

LEVITICUS 20:24, 26

Sanctification goes much deeper than merely conforming to rules or regulations. It involves aligning our spirit with the Spirit of Christ in us. It's not holiness by externalism but rather a holiness that stems from within and affects the external. First John 2:15 tells us, "Do not love the world nor the things in the world. If anyone loves the world, the love of the Father is not in him."

In today's verses, we read God's instructions to the Israelites who were headed into a land of plenty—and a land of temptation. In that land would be the Canaanites, Hittites, Amorites, Jebusites, and others who wouldn't be living according to God's standards. God knew that when His people reached their destiny, they would be surrounded by people who thought and believed differently.

As believers, we exist in a world where others don't align with God's heart. When God tells us not to love the world, He's not sentencing us to a life of boredom. Rather, He's warning us not to adopt the worldview that's out of step with His standards and therefore lose the manifestation of His sanctifying work in us.

Friend, perhaps you're not seeing God's supernatural hand in your life because you're too tied to this world and its way of thinking. To experience the fullness of God's sanctifying power within, we need to consecrate ourselves to Him. In other words, God responds to our decision to become consecrated, holy, and set apart. He doesn't force us to make that decision. But if and when you do, you'll experience the amazing power of God changing things around, preparing the way, or working through you.

———

God, help me not be swayed by a culture that doesn't abide by Your standards. Help me stay encouraged, believing fully that I am set apart for You. Amen.

Inside-Out Transformation

May the God of peace Himself sanctify you entirely; and
may your spirit and soul and body be preserved complete,
without blame at the coming of our Lord Jesus Christ.

1 THESSALONIANS 5:23

Too many Christians want to access God's power over sins in their lives without being truly transformed within. God starts with the spirit because our spirit is the part of our being united with His Spirit in us.

When God says He wants to sanctify us entirely, that's another way of saying we need to be totally transformed. It's the process of spiritual growth by which He progressively makes us more like Jesus Christ. It begins the moment we're saved and will continue until the day we die.

Notice the order of transformation in today's verse. When God strengthens and matures us in our spirit, then our soul (by which we are conscious of ourselves) and our body (through which we engage with the outside world) will fall in line. It's an inside-out process. And this order is all-important because it means that outward performance alone will never get us where God wants us to be.

The story is told of a little girl who turned to her mother one Sunday and said, "Mommy, the preacher's sermon confused me. He said God is bigger than we are. And he also said God lives in us. Is that true?"

Her mother said, "Yes."

"Well," said the girl, "if God is bigger than us and He lives in us, shouldn't He show through?"

We all should ponder the little girl's pragmatic question in our own walk with *Jehovah Mekoddishkem*. This is exactly what God wants to do—reveal Himself, His glory, and His holiness through our everyday lives. He delivers you and me from the bondage of sin today through the sacrifice of Jesus Christ—to sanctify us so that in our intimacy with Him, He can "show through" us to others.

———

God*, transform me from within so that I am made more like Christ. I want You to show through me to others in my daily life. Amen.*

EXPERIENCE *Jehovah Mekoddishkem*

FOCUS SCRIPTURE

As for you, speak to the sons of Israel, saying, "You shall surely observe My sabbaths; for this is a sign between Me and you throughout your generations, that you may know that I am the LORD who sanctifies you" (Exodus 31:13).

What evidence of your transformation from within have you noticed that lets you know you've been sanctified by the Lord?

_____

_____

_____

FOR REFLECTION

Describe a time you encountered God as *Jehovah Mekoddishkem*.

_____

_____

_____

Which characteristic of *Jehovah Mekoddishkem* draws you closer to God? Why?

_____

_____

_____

Which message from the devotions this week did you most need—and why?

_____

_____

_____

PERSONAL PRAYER

I praise You, *Jehovah Mekoddishkem*, for…

_____

_____

_____

Forgive me, *Jehovah Mekoddishkem*, when I…

_____

_____

_____

I'm grateful to You, *Jehovah Mekoddishkem*, for…

_____

_____

_____

Jehovah Mekoddishkem, today I need Your help to…

_____

_____

_____

The word *kaddesh* ("to sanctify") appears hundreds of times in the Bible, but the compound connection of this word with *Jehovah* appears only twice—in Leviticus 20:7-8 and in Exodus 31:13. It's sometimes condensed to *Jehovah M'kaddesh*.

Praises Before the Wilderness

I will sing to the LORD, for He is highly exalted; the horse and its rider He has hurled into the sea. The LORD is my strength and song, and He has become my salvation.

EXODUS 15:1-2

None of us enjoy a perfect, pain-free life. We all need to be made well because of something that's broken in our bodies, emotions, or situations. We may need to be healed of pain from the past or anguish in the present. Many people need healing from the anxiety of uncertainty about their future. Whatever the case, the need for healing in most people's lives is real and deep.

The name of God we'll look at now focuses specifically on God's power to heal. That name is *Jehovah Rapha*, "the Lord who heals." The revelation of this strong name comes on the heels of a great miracle—God parted the waters of the Red Sea and then flooded the path of the Israelites' enemies behind them.

As might be expected, the Israelites broke out into praise following this miraculous intervention by God. Today's Scripture gives us a glimpse into the people's hearts. They were on an emotional and spiritual high, exultantly confident in God as He had just demonstrated Himself before them. But then we read that the Israelites "went out into the wilderness of Shur" (Exodus 15:22). Having just come through water, they hit dry land—*very* dry land. The only way for them to get from Egypt to Canaan, their place of deliverance, was through the wilderness. And they were not happy.

The same is true for our lives. Sometimes the discomfort of the wilderness is the only way we can get to where God is taking us. It's vital to understand that the Lord who heals is not with us only in the miracle moment; *Jehovah Rapha* is also with us when we hit the dry land of illness, grief, or physical pain. The question is, will we praise and trust Him in our wilderness?

———

God, *I need not wait for the victory, for the healing to experience Your presence. You are here as I struggle, stumble, and grieve. You are my healer. Amen.*

A Reason for the Wilderness

There He made for them a statute and
regulation, and there He tested them.

EXODUS 15:25

Tests and trials are designed to do two things: They demonstrate whether we've
been paying attention to the lessons we've learned, and they give God opportunities to reveal something new about Himself, which develops our character and
strengthens our faith.

When I was in school, my teachers tested me only on what they had covered in
class. A test reveals whether the student was paying attention when the information was delivered. The Israelites have come through the water of the Red Sea only
to run out of water in the desert. And when they do encounter water in Marah, it
is bitter and unhealthy. Even though the information God had given to the Israelites three days before was that He was bigger and more powerful than water, they
doubted a solution would come. Their attitude of gratitude turned into grumbling.

God was leading them into their test to see if they were paying attention in
class. It's important to note that God hadn't led them outside of His will. Remember that, friend. You could be in God's will and still hit the dry land of not having
a job, experiencing emotional turmoil, or even facing death. The night before Jesus
was crucified, He prayed to His Father, asking Him not to take us out of the world
but to keep us safe *in* the world. The goal, Jesus realized, wasn't to steer around difficulty but to navigate safely through it.

That's why He sometimes doesn't deliver us from certain situations. Take heart.
God has a purpose for our problems. Your journey through the wilderness is as
important as your arrival to God's destination for you. Take comfort in your pain
or predicament so that you can rejoice in *Jehovah Rapha* even when the healing
hasn't come.

———

*God, for too long I've thought my difficult times were punishment or my fault, but You have
a purpose for the pain and for the problems. I rest in this truth with gratitude. Amen.*

Your Heart Condition

The LORD showed him a tree; and he threw it into the waters,
and the waters became sweet.

EXODUS 15:25

When I go to the doctor's office for my annual exam every summer, he asks, "Tony, how are you feeling?"

Most years, I answer, "I'm feeling fine."

But that's not the end of my appointment. The doctor doesn't take my word for it. Instead, he attaches electronic probes all over my body and has me run on a treadmill because he wants to know the real condition of my heart.

Friend, you can say your faith is fine, but God doesn't simply take your word for it. He tests you because He wants to know the real condition of your heart. He tests you because He's getting ready to do something amazing and wants to know you're looking to Him for your strength and hope.

I often hear people say, "God won't put more on me than I can bear." Let me debunk that myth right now. In 2 Corinthians 1:8, Paul wrote, "We do not want you to be unaware, brethren, of our affliction…that we were burdened excessively, beyond our strength, *so that we despaired even of life.*" Many problems are beyond what *we* can bear. That's the point. It is God alone who somehow ultimately "raises the dead" for us and becomes real in those trials.

After Moses cried out about the bitter waters of Marah to the Lord, God resolved the problem with a tree. That's definitely an unorthodox way to purify water, but sometimes unorthodox ways are how God shows us who's in charge.

At Marah, God reminds the Israelites and you and me that even though His methods are beyond our conventions, He's always the source we're to depend on for healing, provision, and life.

———

God, heal me from my heart condition of doubt. Thank You for Your steadfast love and for how You turn my bitter waters sweet again and again. Amen.

Commands and Statutes

He said, "If you will give earnest heed to the voice of the LORD your God,
and do what is right in His sight, and give ear to His commandments, and
keep all His statutes, I will put none of the diseases on you which I have
put on the Egyptians; for I, the LORD [*Jehovah*], am your healer [*Rapha*]."

EXODUS 15:26

D o you feel stuck in a bitter place? Just as God instructed Moses to throw a stick into the bitter water, He may instruct you to do something that doesn't seem to add up. But when you follow His commands, you'll discover that He can turn anything into something far better than you could have ever imagined.

After God taught the Israelites and revealed to them His name *Jehovah Rapha*, He immediately took them to Elim, where there was more than enough of a good thing for everyone. Exodus 15:27 says, "There were twelve springs of water and seventy date palms, and they camped there beside the waters."

The Israelites get to the abundant refreshment of Elim only by going through the test at Marah and only after they meet *Jehovah Rapha*. When you learn the lesson of Marah and align your thoughts, heart, and actions under God, He would love to take you to Elim, where you can enjoy your own private spring. The book of John tells us that this is your destiny if you will but seek Christ as your Lord and Savior.

And you *yourself* will be a spring (John 7:38-39)! You will experience health in your own mind, body, and relationships and become a blessing that God uses to bring health to others. Later in this devotional journey, we'll meet the Living Water as the Holy Spirit.

Even in the midst of our deepest pain, God has a way to sweeten the waters and to use the pain and suffering to make us stronger. He is *Jehovah Rapha,* and He longs to refresh you.

———

God, healing is possible in Your power. Give me eyes and a heart to witness what Your healing in this season looks like. I praise You, Jehovah Rapha. Amen.

EXPERIENCE *Jehovah Rapha*

FOCUS SCRIPTURE

Bless the LORD, O my soul, and forget none of His benefits; who pardons all your iniquities, who heals all your diseases (Psalm 103:2-3).

What physical, emotional, spiritual, or relational healing have you experienced from the hand of *Jehovah Rapha*?

_____

_____

_____

FOR REFLECTION

Describe a time you encountered God as *Jehovah Rapha*.

_____

_____

_____

Which characteristic of *Jehovah Rapha* draws you closer to God? Why?

_____

_____

_____

Which message from the devotions this week did you most need—and why?

_____

_____

_____

PERSONAL PRAYER

I praise You, *Jehovah Rapha*, for…

_____

_____

_____

Forgive me, *Jehovah Rapha*, when I…

_____

_____

_____

I'm grateful to You, *Jehovah Rapha*, for…

_____

_____

_____

Jehovah Rapha, today I need Your help to…

_____

_____

_____

The name *Jehovah Rapha* is not a guarantee we'll never have health issues. That isn't the sickness God is speaking of when He reveals Himself as *Jehovah Rapha*. He's talking about the diseases He put on the Egyptians because of their rebellion against Him. You won't have to face those diseases when your heart is aligned under God and His ways.

Rescued from Above

I will cry to God Most High, to God who accomplishes all things for me.

PSALM 57:2

On August 5, 2010, after a cave-in, 33 Chilean miners were trapped 2,300 feet underground in a copper and gold mine just outside a small town called Copiapó. They were imprisoned in a seemingly impenetrable fortress of rock.

It's bad enough to be in a pit, but it's even more discouraging when you can't tell if anyone above is helping you. The rescuers were discouraged, too, when they'd heard nothing from the miners for more than two weeks. Then one day a note was taped to one of their drill bits as it resurfaced. The miners were alive. Through a small tube, the rescuers provided the miners with food, water, light, medicine, and communication equipment. It was the hope they all needed to press on.

Maybe it seems that life has caved in on you spiritually, financially, relationally, or emotionally. You see no way out. Like the trapped miners, you aren't even sure anyone above knows where you are. Friend, meet *El Elyon,* "the Most High God." He is the One who looks down from on high to see your every need. Trusting Him becomes a lifeline. Praising Him reminds you who is responsible for your hope.

After all 33 miners were miraculously saved, one man shared that they had gathered to pray. They called on God's name for help, and they gave Him glory.

Knowing God's names doesn't prevent life's negative realities. But knowing God intimately through His names does provide a sustaining hope in the darkness. Hope comes to us in the dark because God is aware of our plight and working on our behalf.

No matter what kind of pit you're in, you can call out to *El Elyon.* You can trust that He is the One above who has a plan for your rescue and your salvation.

———

God, You are the One above me who sends down the provision I need to survive. You are the One above who doesn't forget that I am below and in need of hope and light. Amen.

God's Odds

Blessed be Abram of God Most High [*El Elyon*], possessor
of heaven and earth; and blessed be God Most High [*El
Elyon*], who has delivered your enemies into your hand.

GENESIS 14:19-20

Once again, we discover a new name for God because He's meeting the needs of His children. A battle of nine human kings—four against five—is raging when Abram hears that his nephew Lot has been taken prisoner. Abram rounds up his best 318 men and travels a great distance to fight the larger armies.

It's clear that no one should have messed with Abram. Though the odds were against him, he trusted that God was above the battle and even the kings. And God was victorious. After the battle, the king of Sodom came to Abram and brought with him Melchizedek, the king of Salem. Transliterated, the name Salem aligns with the Hebrew word *shalem*, which means "peace." This king of peace brought bread and wine to Abram. He came as the priest of *El Elyon*, God Most High, and blessed Abram with the words in today's key passage.

Abram responded, "I have sworn to the LORD God Most High [*El Elyon*], possessor of heaven and earth" (verse 22). Both the king and Abram acknowledge and honor who's really in charge.

Most likely some people of wealth, power, or influence sit pretty high in your world. Yet no matter how high they are, *El Elyon* is higher still. *El Elyon* is the maker of heaven and earth. And if those people seek to intimidate you, they don't have the final say. Your recourse is to call on *El Elyon*, who is higher, stronger, and more influential than your boss, doctor, spouse, political leader, banker, or anyone who's trying to hold you down.

In your situation, don't look at your odds or the status of another. Look to *El Elyon*. He is the only one with the final say.

God, *keep me from weighing the odds or sizing up obstacles and calling them insurmountable. The odds are in my favor when I have favor in Your eyes. Amen.*

Credit the Creator

Abram said to the king of Sodom, "I have sworn to the
LORD God Most High, possessor of heaven and earth, that
I will not take a thread or a sandal thong or anything that is
yours, for fear you would say, 'I have made Abram rich.'"

GENESIS 14:22-23

One of the many great blessings of being aligned with the God Most High is that you are able to taste the goodness of a conflict won or a problem solved as you give the praise and glory to the One above it all.

Abram's intrinsic understanding of God's character and holiness comes at the end of the battle story. Following Melchizedek's blessing and Abram's response—he gave Melchizedek a tenth (a tithe)—a revealing verbal exchange occurs between the king of Sodom and Abram. It's featured in today's passage.

The king of Sodom ruled one of the nations that Abram had delivered. Knowing Abram was a force with which to be reckoned, he sought to strike a deal. He asked Abram to give him the people he had recovered, and in exchange, Abram could keep all of the loot. He and his men could profit from the rescue.

The problem with this pitch is that the king of Sodom ignores the fact that he had been captured himself. He was suggesting a 50/50 split when he actually owed his life and the victory to Abram and God. Abram knew the king wanted to parade the captured people back into his city so he could claim them as servants and slaves. This king was vying for credit that belonged to God alone.

So adamant was Abram against the king of Sodom stealing any of God's glory that he told him he wouldn't even take "a thread or a sandal thong" just so the king couldn't claim that he had contributed to Abram's success. *El Elyon* had won the battle, and *El Elyon* would receive the praise due Him.

May this be our response when Satan entices us to take credit for the victories *El Elyon* ushers into our lives.

———

God, forgive me for whenever I've taken credit for Your victories. May I never forget that Your hands deliver me from my enemies and that, from on high, You win the battle. Amen.

God Is Your Source

I am the LORD, that is My name; I will not give My glory to another.

ISAIAH 42:8

The spiritual principle of the Source versus the resource came to me in my late thirties as I studied God's Word. It made a revolutionary difference in my choices, my level of worry, and my planning.

Friend, if you fully grasp this truth, it will change everything for you: *God is your Source. Everything else is a resource.* Melchizedek underscored this when he pointed out that Abram conquered his enemies because *El Elyon* had delivered them into his hands.

We have only one Source. And one of the worst things you or I could ever do is treat a resource as if it were our Source. That means that whatever resource in your life is messing with you, it doesn't have the last word. God can find another resource through which to bless you. He has more than one way to accomplish His purposes.

Understanding the power of *El Elyon* is a freeing experience. Sometimes when I take the interstate to downtown Dallas, some lanes are closed due to construction. Cars have blocked me in, and traffic is sitting still. But because I've lived in Dallas for so long, I just take the first exit I come to. I know other routes to my destination. The interstate is only one resource on my pathway—it's not the only resource.

Situations and circumstances in life can have a similar effect. They seem to block our progress, and we can feel stalled on the path to our destiny. But let this truth sink in today: Nothing can block you when you're paired up with *El Elyon*. He will get you to your destiny no matter who or what seems to stand in your way.

———

God, *You have many ways to take me from point A to point B. Instead of fretting when I can't see up ahead, I will trust Your view from above to lead me in purpose. Amen.*

EXPERIENCE *El Elyon*

FOCUS SCRIPTURE

They remembered that God was their rock, and the Most High God their Redeemer (Psalm 78:35).

When has the Most High God been your rock and redeemer?

_____

_____

_____

FOR REFLECTION

Describe a time you encountered God as *El Elyon*.

_____

_____

_____

Which characteristic of *El Elyon* draws you closer to God? Why?

_____

_____

_____

Which message from the devotions this week did you most need—and why?

_____

_____

_____

PERSONAL PRAYER

I praise You, *El Elyon*, for…

_____

_____

_____

Forgive me, *El Elyon*, when I…

_____

_____

_____

I'm grateful to You, *El Elyon*, for…

_____

_____

_____

El Elyon, today I need Your help to…

_____

_____

_____

When we look at the meaning of the name *El Elyon*, we need to remember that *El* is the abbreviated form of *Elohim*. *Elohim* is the name given to God in creation, referring to His power: "In the beginning God [*Elohim*] created the heavens and the earth" (Genesis 1:1). When *El* is combined with *Elyon*, the compound connection refers to God as the highest or the most.

God Takes His Covenants Seriously

The LORD said to Abram, "Go forth from your country…to
the land which I will show you; and I will make you a great
nation, and I will bless you, and make your name great."

GENESIS 12:1-3

El Shaddai is one of my favorite names of God. It's a powerful compound connection of *El* ("God") and *Shaddai* ("almighty, sufficient"). Soon we'll look at when we're introduced to this name in Genesis 17, but today I want to highlight this truth: God will do what He says He will do simply because He is faithful to His promises and covenant.

When Abram was 75 years old, God told him He had a special plan for him and a special blessing. In fact, God's covenants always involve blessing. A blessing is God's favor expressed to you and through you to others to bring Him glory.

God's covenant with Abram is to make him a great nation by first giving him an heir. This is great news to elderly Abram. Yet when God said He was going to bless him, it wasn't merely a promise to bring about good things to him. The rest of today's passage is "And so you shall be a blessing; and I will bless those who bless you" (Genesis 12:2-3). A blessing is never only what God does to you; a blessing is what God does to you so that it might flow through you to others.

Let's recap today's truths. God is faithful. His blessing for you isn't just about you. Also important: God is in charge of fulfilling the covenant. Our job is to obey and wait as long as it takes. We never have to wonder, question, or doubt whether God will follow through. Keep that in mind as we read on. Believing God is faithful is foundational for your faith, your faithfulness, and your future.

——

God, I'm not always good at waiting and obeying. But I trust You are in charge. You bless me with Your faithfulness. May I be worthy and faithful as I wait with confidence. Amen.

When We Try to Take Over

Sarai, Abram's wife had borne him no children, and she had an Egyptian maid
whose name was Hagar. So Sarai said to Abram, "Now behold, the LORD has
prevented me from bearing children. Please go in to my maid; perhaps I will
obtain children through her"...He went in to Hagar, and she conceived.

GENESIS 16:1-2, 4

This Bible story reads like a dramedy as Abram and Sarai become impatient
and try to fulfill the covenant on their own. It would be a comedy except it
hits close to home for many of us who have also tried to take over God's role in
one of our situations.

A few years after the covenant, Abram has begun to doubt that this promise
will ever come to fruition. He questions God: "O Lord GOD, what will You give
me, since I am childless, and the heir of my house is Eliezer of Damascus?" (Genesis 15:2). Mistake one.

Abram assumes that since God hasn't given him an offspring, the heir God
intends to use to fulfill the promise of making him a great nation will be someone
merely born in his house instead of through him physically. God clarifies that the
heir will be a child born of Abram, yet Abram doubts once again. Not only that,
but Sarai blames God for not fulfilling the promise: "The LORD has prevented me
from bearing children." So she and Abram decide that Abram should impregnate
their maid Hagar. Mistake two.

If you're familiar with the rest of the story, you know how devastating their second decision was, not only for the people at that time but for the nations that have
followed Ishmael (the father of the Arabs), born of this union between Abram and
Hagar. The Arabs and Israelites have been in conflict ever since.

So much heartache is caused when we take control rather than surrender to
God. If you're about to meddle in God's plan, step back and wait on Him. Don't
block the blessings He has in store for you and for those who will be blessed
through you. Instead, praise His name while you wait.

———

*God, Your way is so much better. In this life season, help me let go of control so that my big
ideas don't get in the way of Your eternal plans. Amen.*

God Is Your Source

I am God Almighty [*El Shaddai*]; walk before Me, and
be blameless. I will establish My covenant between
Me and you, and I will multiply you exceedingly.

GENESIS 17:1-2

When God introduces Himself to Abram as *El Shaddai* in the context of a covenant, Abram is 99 years old. God has been watching the antics of Abram and Sarai as they scramble to make His promise happen in their limited wisdom.

You may think God is too slow to meet your need as promised. Maybe you think He's taking too long to help you find a mate, fix your marriage, change your child, solidify your career, or give you some other breakthrough. At some point we've all felt at least a bit like that.

Yet it's precisely in those times that God reminds us just who He is. At Abram's moment of deepest doubt, God told him His name was *El Shaddai*. The name comes from the root word *shad*, which literally means "breast." *Shad* is sometimes used to signify the supply of nourishment. When a woman nurses her baby, she supplies what that baby needs to live. The name *El Shaddai*, when coupled with its root meaning, presents the image of God supplying the nourishment needed to sustain life.

Abram and Sarai have proven their impatience and their bad judgment, so God has to remind them who's in charge. Remember, our Source is different from our resources. If you're wondering how even God could work out His covenant in your circumstances, take a pause before you delay the progress of the promise with some wild, human plan B. Surrender to *El Shaddai*—He is both the creator and sustainer of life. He loves to manifest Himself in the context of the impossible. You don't have to figure it out because He will work it out—just as we witness His doing for Abram and Sarai.

God, *Your power and wisdom have no limits. You bless me with provision as You covenant with me through Your Son. Thank You for Your love and Your promises. Amen.*

A New Covenant

As for Me, behold, My covenant is with you, and you will
be the father of a multitude of nations. No longer shall your
name be called Abram, but your name shall be Abraham;
for I have made you the father of a multitude of nations.

GENESIS 17:4-5

After hearing God's new name, *El Shaddai*, Abram finally fell on his face before the God who can create life and sustain it. And as evidence of this covenant, Abram got a new name himself—Abraham.

God told him that not only would he be the father of one heir but the father of a "multitude of nations." The name Abraham literally means "exalted father." God changed Abram's name to fit the promise. And within a year, Abraham and Sarah had a son together.

Are you tired and discouraged? Have you messed up along the way by trying to help God but only made things worse? If that's you, I encourage you to focus on the name *El Shaddai*. Yes, you may have waited a very long time, but you're still here, just as Abraham and Sarah were still there, and God can still supply.

If you're stranded on what seems to be a dead-end road, look to *El Shaddai* to be with you as you wait for your breakthrough. Friend, the lessons we've learned in this story and in this journey through God's names will prepare your heart to fully surrender to the covenant between God and those who have trusted Christ for their salvation. These covenants from thousands of years ago relate to the most important covenant in your life today.

Put your hope in *El Shaddai*. He knows you, He loves you, and He will sustain you when you trust Him to fulfill His promises in and through you. You, too, will see the fruit of your belief—either in this world or in the next. It's a promise from a God who says, "Those who hope in me will not be disappointed" (Isaiah 49:23 NIV).

———

God, *You want my heart and not my human solutions. You want my trust and not my tangents. I will stop interfering and start surrendering, Almighty God. Amen.*

EXPERIENCE *El Shaddai*

FOCUS SCRIPTURE

He who dwells in the shelter of the Most High will abide in the shadow of the Almighty [*Shaddai*]. I will say to the LORD, "My refuge and my fortress, My God, in whom I trust!" (Psalm 91:1-2).

Describe a time when you learned to trust God Almighty.

_____

_____

_____

FOR REFLECTION

Describe a time you encountered God as *El Shaddai*.

_____

_____

_____

Which characteristic of *El Shaddai* draws you closer to God? Why?

_____

_____

_____

Which message from the devotions this week did you most need—and why?

_____

_____

_____

PERSONAL PRAYER

I praise You, *El Shaddai*, for…

_____

_____

_____

Forgive me, *El Shaddai*, when I…

_____

_____

_____

I'm grateful to You, *El Shaddai*, for…

_____

_____

_____

El Shaddai, today I need Your help to…

_____

_____

_____

El Shaddai the name appears seven times in the Old Testament, yet God is also referenced solely as *Shaddai* another 41 times. God introduces Himself to Abram (and to us) as *El Shaddai* in the context of a covenant. This covenant is a formal, official agreement God makes with us. The fact that *El Shaddai* is introduced to us in the context of God's covenant is no small thing as God takes His covenants seriously.

JESUS

Being found in appearance as a man,
He humbled Himself by becoming obedient
to the point of death, even death on a
cross. For this reason also, God highly
exalted Him, and bestowed on Him the
name which is above every name.

PHILIPPIANS 2:8-9

Name Above Every Name

When you get to know the names of Jesus, you discover on whom you can base your truth. He will not forsake you when you seek Him with your whole heart and mind. There is power in the name of Jesus.

John 14:13-15 emphasizes this as well. Jesus says, "Whatever you ask in My name, that will I do, so that the Father may be glorified in the Son. If you ask Me anything in My name, I will do it. If you love Me, you will keep My commandments."

As you get to know and understand some of the names and descriptions of Jesus throughout this next section and submit yourself to His authority, you'll discover how to tap into the power of the one and only Jesus, your Lord, your Christ, and your God. When God became flesh, He sent the Son and gave Him the name above every name and the power to conquer death.

In this journey together, we'll encounter Jesus as someone who was there at the very beginning of the world and was born as fully God and fully human to walk among God's creation. We also experience Him as the one who asked the Father to send the Holy Spirit, the Helper, to be an ever-present power within believers.

Jesus is "before all things, and in Him all things hold together. He is also head of the body, the church; and He is the beginning, the firstborn from the dead, so that He Himself will come to have first place in everything" (Colossians 1:17-18). Friend, if you're going to close your prayers with "in Jesus's name," make sure that isn't merely a tag line. Make sure you're honoring the One who is given the name above every name and has first place in your heart.

God *with* Us

All this took place to fulfill what was spoken by the Lord
through the prophet: "Behold, the virgin shall be with
child and shall bear a Son, and they shall call His name
Immanuel," which translated means, "God with us."

MATTHEW 1:22-23

A master key is designed to unlock multiple doors—and you have been given the master key to God: Jesus. He reveals to us the heart, mind, and nature of God. Only through Jesus do we get to know God and discover the depth of His power and the fullness of His love. With Jesus, we have gained entrance into the presence of God and access to understanding His full character.

No other name of Jesus reflects the nature of God's heart toward us like the name Immanuel, "God with us." The context of that meaning can be found only in Isaiah, which Matthew referenced in our passage today. During the time of Isaiah's writing about Immanuel, God's people were being attacked by their enemy. In the midst of their fear, anxiety, and dread, God showed up and told King Ahaz that He would give him a sign of victory. This would be no ordinary sign, either. A virgin would bear a son. It was promised that when this sign came about, it would be an ongoing reminder of God's presence with them, despite what was attacking them.

Immanuel isn't merely a name to remember at Christmastime as we sing carols and drink hot chocolate. Immanuel is a name of comfort during the worst of times. It's a reminder that whatever enemies or problems you're facing, enduring, or exhausted by, God is with you. The birth of Jesus Christ is not only the introduction of our Savior into this world, but also the introduction of God's promise of victory and His presence in the midst of a painful reality we all know far too well.

Live your day remembering that you have what you need to open the door to God's presence.

———

Jesus, I hold Your name dear because it's the name that says You came near. With love, sacrifice, humility, and a plan for our salvation, You came to be with Your creation. Amen.

The Unique Birth of a King

God was pleased to have all His fullness dwell in Him.

COLOSSIANS 1:19 HCSB

A new birth in a royal family usually prompts great pomp and fanfare—massive media saturation and a lot of celebration. But not in the case of Jesus. He came as a king, and He could have been born in a castle, yet the babe was born in a barn to parents who were both unknown and poor. He arrived with little worldly notice.

Why should we give attention to Jesus's birth? Because heaven's own heart had beat in the womb of a young woman for the previous nine months. Most likely just a young teenager herself, Jesus's mother, Mary, was full of a faith far greater than expected for the years she'd known. Out of her body came God's omnipotence covered in humanity's limitations.

Her child was flesh, bones, sinew, and blood. Yet He was also the perfection of deity. He felt hunger because He was fully human, yet He would later feed five thousand from little because He was fully God (Luke 9:10-17). He grew thirsty because He was fully human, yet He would one day walk on water because He was fully God (John 6:16-21). His was a unique birth because His destiny and rule were to be like no others.

As Messiah and King over all, Jesus has already established the rules of His reign. He has set the tone through His life. In His kingdom, neither race nor gender nor wealth nor social status determines our place in Him (Galatians 3:28). We may not relate to a ruler or a king, but we can relate to the struggles, needs, and losses the baby of Bethlehem would face.

What a gift that God gave us a Savior we could understand from the very beginning.

———

Jesus, thank You that even though You created kings, dominions, rulers, and authorities, You also created a way to spend time with someone like me. Amen.

God Revealed

He is the image of the invisible God, the firstborn of all creation.

COLOSSIANS 1:15

When we talk about Jesus—Immanuel—we're not just talking about a man who lived and died on earth. This is God in the flesh. Over and over again in Scripture, we witness Jesus manifesting the fullness of deity, which is God alone. Even when it comes to the names of God, Jesus exemplifies and embodies them. Let's look at a few examples of "God with us."

- In the Old Testament, God is called *Elohim*, which means the Creator God. The New Testament tells us that everything has been created by Jesus (Colossians 1:16).

- One of God's names is *Jehovah Rohi*, which means the Lord is our shepherd. Jesus came to us as the Good Shepherd whose sheep know His voice (John 10:4, 11).

- Another name of God is *El Elyon*, meaning the Lord who is high and mighty. Jesus sits at the right hand of the Father, high above (Ephesians 1:20-21).

Jesus is God with us in every way. Jesus came so that we may know God more fully and experience His power more completely as He deals with our sins and our circumstances. If you want to get to know the names of Jesus, get to know the names of God like you did in the first third of this journey, because Jesus is the fulfillment of every name of God. And He has come as Immanuel in order to reveal God to us. Should you ever become confused about who God is and what He's like, all you have to do is remember Immanuel.

From the beginning of the world to its end, there's no place you can look and not see God revealed through Jesus.

———

Jesus, help me know the heart of God in a way and at a depth I've never known before. I seek and am thankful for Your closeness. May I be intentional to draw near to You. Amen.

When We Have the Son

He who did not spare His own Son, but delivered Him over for
us all, how will He not also with Him freely give us all things?

ROMANS 8:32

There's a story of a wealthy man who had lost his beloved son, and then later he himself died. Over his lifetime, he had accumulated many expensive possessions, which, following his death, were to be auctioned off at an estate sale. Knowing of the man's exquisite taste in fine treasures, hundreds of people showed up.

To everyone's surprise, the auctioneer started the sale by holding up a cheaply framed painting, saying, "The first piece is this portrait of the man's only son. Do I have a bid?" The room was awkwardly still even after he asked for bids again. And again.

Finally, from the back of the room, an elderly man said, "Sir, I was the servant of the man who died, and if no one will buy the portrait of his son, I want to know if I can have it."

After a last inquiry was met with silence, the auctioneer said to the servant, "Yes, sir, the painting is yours."

The servant walked forward to take hold of the portrait. Looking lovingly at the boy's image, he then tucked it under his arm and walked to the back of the room. To everyone's shock, the auctioneer then banged his gavel and said, "The auction is now over."

Everyone was outraged. Someone yelled, "But I'm here for the pieces of value. Where are they?"

The auctioneer replied, "The father valued his son so highly that he stipulated that whoever took his son's portrait would inherit everything."

Friend, how often are we like those buyers who place value entirely on the things of the world? When we abide with Jesus, we gain access to all the Father has for us. The one who cherishes the Son has everything and honors the Father.

Jesus, forgive me for whenever I have prioritized the world over You. I humble my heart before You today and commit to showing my love for You through faithfulness. Amen.

Experience *Immanuel*

FOCUS SCRIPTURE

A child will be born to us, a son will be given to us; and the government will rest on His shoulders; and His name will be called Wonderful Counselor, Mighty God, Eternal Father, Prince of Peace (Isaiah 9:6).

What do you cherish most about Immanuel, "God with us," coming into the world as a child?

_____

_____

_____

FOR REFLECTION

Describe a time you encountered God as Immanuel.

_____

_____

_____

Which characteristic of Immanuel draws you closer to God? Why?

_____

_____

_____

Which message from the devotions this week did you most need—and why?

_____

_____

_____

PERSONAL PRAYER

I praise You, Immanuel, for…

_____

_____

_____

Forgive me, Immanuel, when I…

_____

_____

_____

I'm grateful to You, Immanuel, for…

_____

_____

_____

Immanuel, today I need Your help to…

_____

_____

_____

The theological term for deity emptied into humanity is *kenosis*. On that first Christmas morning, we had a baby in a manger who had created His own mother. We had a baby in a stable who had created the donkeys, sheep, and shepherds who surrounded Him and made the hay on which He lay. On the day Jesus entered our earth as a baby, God poured Himself into flesh. He became Immanuel—"God with us."

Your First, Last, and Only

"I am the Alpha and the Omega," says the Lord God,
"who is and who was and who is to come, the Almighty."

REVELATION 1:8

Because knowing *A* to *Z* serves as the foundation upon which we can understand all words, the English alphabet was one of the first things most of us in the English-speaking world were taught. These words then comprise our thoughts, and the communication of those thoughts becomes the bedrock for all knowledge.

Because we know how important language and words are, we'll often use the phrase *from A to Z* to indicate the fullness of a task or topic. This isn't merely referring to the letters in the alphabet. Rather, this phrase references the completeness of whatever point is being made.

Now, what "A to Z" is in the English language, "alpha and omega" is in Greek. *Alpha* is the first letter of the Greek alphabet, and *omega* is the last. When Jesus lived on earth, He lived in a Greek-speaking world. He understood the significance of *alpha* and *omega*. Just as *from A to Z* signifies the completeness of communication, fullness of knowledge, and clarity of thought, the phrase *alpha and omega* symbolized the same for the culture in which Jesus lived. Thus, when He said He is the Alpha and the Omega, He was declaring that He Himself is the complete knowledge base for all life.

By saying this, He also declared that He is the living God. We know this because God referred to Himself in the same way in the Old Testament: "Thus says the LORD, the King of Israel and his Redeemer, the LORD of hosts: 'I am the first and I am the last, and there is no God besides Me'" (Isaiah 44:6).

Today, let yourself rest in the truth that you don't need to look further than Jesus. He is your first and last and only source for knowledge, hope, and salvation.

———

Jesus, *You are above all, over all, before all, and after all. You are the sum total as well as the details in between. You are my first and last everything, Lord. Amen.*

The Last Word

He brought about in Christ...far above all rule and authority
and power and dominion, and every name that is named,
not only in this age but also in the one to come.

EPHESIANS 1:20-21

When we view Jesus as a great historical figure who healed people and did good, but we don't allow Him to inform every aspect of our lives, we lack the wisdom and knowledge to make productive and healthy choices. Because they give Him a nod on Sundays but don't look to Him as the ruler over all, far too many believers struggle just to get by rather than live out the abundant life Jesus died to provide.

Jesus isn't the *A* to only the *G* in our lives. He isn't to be taken into consideration some of the time. He is the ultimate Alpha and Omega, the beginning and the end. Jesus is above all. Every part of your life and mind is to be connected, plugged into, and in sync with Jesus Christ. He is the revelation of God from heaven to earth. His job is to bring the truth of heaven to bear on our lives on earth. What Jesus says, goes. At least that's how it should be.

Jesus is the final word. Period.

Many of our arguments, dilemmas, and struggles last too long. They become run-on sentences in our story, because Jesus isn't acknowledged as the Alpha and the Omega. We tend to go to Him only when we need Him to bail us out in the messy middle. But that's not why He came.

Jesus came so we might have life to full capacity from beginning to end (John 10:10). That happens only when we align our lives under His overarching truth. We access His strength when we access His truth. We grasp His peace when we grasp His truth. We enjoy His provision when we employ His truth. We experience His power only when He has the final say all of our days.

Jesus, *I want to trade my limited life for the abundant life You died to provide. You are the first and last word, and I want You to be my first, last, and only love and truth. Amen.*

Finishing Strong

He said to me, "It is done. I am the Alpha and the Omega,
the beginning and the end. I will give to the one who thirsts
from the spring of the water of life without cost."

REVELATION 21:6

So many of us are tired. Weary. This type of tiredness is known as "losing heart." Life may not be working in your favor, as you see it. Maybe it's your fault that things aren't going well. Or maybe it's someone else's fault. Regardless of the reason, the result is the same: You're worn out. Your hope has waned, and your fervency has fizzled.

But those who discover the secret of aligning their lives under Jesus's truth can finish the race and fulfill the calling God has created them to live out. Hebrews 12:1-3 explains this:

> Let us run with endurance the race that is set before us, fixing our eyes on Jesus, the author and perfecter of faith, who for the joy set before Him endured the cross, despising the shame, and has sat down at the right hand of the throne of God. For consider Him who has endured such hostility by sinners against Himself, so that you will not grow weary and lose heart.

Even though things are rough right now, don't quit.

You have a race to finish—a figurative race of living the kingdom life for the glory of God and the good of yourself and others. You may have gotten sidelined along the way or detoured by heeding human wisdom, but Jesus came to set you back on track and to sate your thirst from the spring of the water of life. Your body, mind, and spirit need the refreshment that comes from the Alpha and Omega. You have the power to keep going because the Alpha and Omega has the power to both start and finish whatever you might face. You are not left alone in this race, my friend. Not ever.

Jesus, when my hope wanes, I come to You, and my faith is restored. I was never meant to run this race alone. You refresh my hope to persevere with joy. Amen.

Eyes on Him

Peter got out of the boat, and walked on the water and came toward Jesus. But seeing the wind, he became frightened, and beginning to sink, he cried out, "Lord, save me!" Immediately Jesus stretched out His hand and took hold of him, and said to him, "You of little faith, why did you doubt?"

MATTHEW 14:29-31

When you're fixated on something or someone, you've stopped giving attention to anything else. It's not possible to be fixated on multiple things simultaneously. To be fixated on Jesus means you're zeroing in on Him and not on other people and their opinions or even on your own viewpoints.

We have to look to the power that can overcome so that we have the endurance to press on. A great biblical illustration of this is found in Matthew 14:22-31. We read about when a great storm hit the sea, and yet Jesus walked to His disciples on the rough water. The problem was the storm. But when Jesus came to the disciples, He walked on top of the very problem itself. Without getting rid of the storm, He overcame it. He overpowered it.

When Jesus called to Peter to come to Him, Peter was able to overcome the storm himself only when he kept his eyes fixed on Jesus. The moment he took his eyes off Jesus and focused instead on the tumultuous circumstances, he began to sink.

Life is uncertain. Storms arise. In these times, ask yourself, *Where are my spiritual eyes directed?* If you're looking only at your circumstances, they'll overwhelm you. They'll sink you.

Jesus bids you to come to Him in the midst of risky situations. He asks you to step out in faith. But He gives you success only when you keep your eyes focused on Him, the Alpha and the Omega. He is the beginning and the end. He is the author and the finisher. He will get you across the finish line. Whether that's on the rough seas of a struggle or through the parched land of a desert season, you know where to look.

———

Jesus, I will keep my eyes on You instead of on the turbulent waves in my life. In Your power, You overcome the storms that rise. They are nothing in Your presence. Amen.

EXPERIENCE *Alpha and Omega*

FOCUS SCRIPTURE

Behold, I am coming quickly, and My reward is with Me, to render to every man according to what he has done. I am the Alpha and the Omega, the first and the last, the beginning and the end (Revelation 22:12-13).

How does thinking of Jesus as both the beginning and the end give you courage and hope for a trouble you have right now?

_____

_____

_____

FOR REFLECTION

Describe a time you encountered Jesus as the Alpha and Omega.

_____

_____

_____

Which characteristic of the Alpha and Omega draws you closer to Jesus? Why?

_____

_____

_____

Which message from the devotions this week did you most need—and why?

_____

_____

_____

PERSONAL PRAYER

I praise You, Alpha and Omega, for…

_____

_____

_____

Forgive me, Alpha and Omega, when I…

_____

_____

_____

I'm grateful to You, Alpha and Omega, for…

_____

_____

_____

Alpha and Omega, today I need Your help to…

_____

_____

_____

Jesus followed up His claim to the name of Alpha and Omega by adding that He is "the first and the last" (Revelation 22:13). He is the first, the last, and everything in between. This name is a claim to deity. If the God of the Old Testament introduced His identity as being the first and the last, then when Jesus described Himself in the same manner, He was revealing that He is a part of the Godhead.

God Has a House

The earth is the LORD's, and all it contains,
the world, and those who dwell in it.

PSALM 24:1

O ne day when my daughter Chrystal was younger and living at home, she was arguing with me about one of my rules. When I wouldn't relent, she decided to walk away while I was still talking. I quickly asked, "Where do you think you're going?"

She replied, "I'm going to my room!"

To which I said, "That is not your room. It's my room, and I let you sleep in it. And right now, you cannot go there."

Most parents can relate to this scene. And most Christians can relate to Chrystal, because somewhere along the way, we've forgotten these principles as they relate to God. God has a house. It's called His kingdom. God's kingdom is His comprehensive rule over all creation. He gets to run His house His way, and He has chosen to rule through humanity by entrusting us with the responsibility of managing His home.

I call His rule the *kingdom agenda*, and it forms the basis of everything I teach. It can be defined as the visible manifestation of the comprehensive rule of God over every area of life. God created the first human, whose job was to run His house His way. Yet when Adam rebelled against the owner, he turned the management of that creation over to Satan by allowing sin to enter the world.

To reinstate humanity's rule, God had to provide another Adam, known as the "last Adam" (1 Corinthians 15:45, 47). The second Adam would succeed because He—Jesus Christ—would be divine. When John the Baptist announced Jesus's arrival, he phrased it in terms the nation of Israel could understand: "Repent, for the kingdom of heaven is at hand" (Matthew 3:2). It was time, and it *is* time, for everyone to get their homes in order, because the ruler of God's house—the King—is here.

———

Jesus, my heart and my life are under Your kingdom rule. I'm in awe that You have entrusted mankind with managing what is Yours. May I be made worthy of this responsibility, Lord. Amen.

Surrender All

What is man that You take thought of him, and the son of man that
You care for him? Yet You have made him a little lower than God, and
You crown him with glory and majesty! You make him to rule over
the works of Your hands; You have put all things under his feet.

PSALM 8:4-6

When we speak or sing about Jesus, it's often about His redemptive roles—Savior, Lamb, and Immanuel. And while these roles are key, I'm afraid that in focusing so heavily on them, we miss out on much of Jesus's power in our daily lives. The name King makes many people nervous. We don't mind Jesus carrying around the title as long as He's not telling us what to do. Obedience, dependence, and surrender go against what our culture tells us is the way to live. So we resist it.

Friend, I'll cut to the chase here to save you time, confusion, and heartache: God's kingdom is not a democracy. He's not asking for your vote or your permission. God is a monarch. He declares what gets done, how things run, and what the goals of His kingdom will be.

Unless and until we understand and submit to Christ's rightful rule, we won't fully experience His power. If we make our own rules while living in the domain of a ruling King, we should expect to face the consequences. We're slow to make the connection between personal disaster and mounting issues in our life as a result of living according to our own rules, not those of our King. Yet we're quick to call on Jesus as King when we want to be bailed out from our circumstances.

Think about how much more joyful and meaningful our lives could be if we called on Jesus as King *before* every decision, choice, pursuit. What if we bowed to Him as King before breakfast? Give the King your devotion and your day. Give Him your loyalty and your life. If surrendering feels like giving in, so be it. We give in to the King's power so we can live in the King's power.

———

Jesus, I come to You today in advance of a decision I must make. I will heed Your wisdom and guidance. I bow before You as King to submit to Your rule and Your love. Amen.

First Things

Seek first His kingdom and His righteousness,
and all these things will be added to you.

MATTHEW 6:33

A lot of us miss out on what God wants to do in our hearts, relationships, finances, jobs, and circumstances simply because we refuse to put Him first in our thoughts, attitudes, and decisions. We don't worship Jesus as King. It's true that the flesh will push back against His commands, but one way to overcome the flesh is to give Jesus permission to tell you what to do. Then obey Him.

When we seek first God's kingdom and His righteousness, everything else will fall in line. In other words, when you seek the King's rule and honor first, He's got your back. If you want to seek your own will and kingdom, then you'll need to have your own back. You don't get it both ways. Yes, Jesus loves you. Yes, Jesus comforts you. Yes, Jesus provides for you. But Jesus also rules over you. And when you choose to disobey Him, you choose to remove yourself from His kingdom benefits.

Many assume if they just get closer to Jesus, the war between the flesh and the spirit will go away. And while getting relationally closer to Jesus is absolutely critical, obeying Him is just as critical—if not more so. In fact, obedience is a key component of increasing intimacy with our King. Recognizing Him as King is what will get your flesh to succumb to the rule of the spirit. Until you establish who's truly in charge, you'll wind up making all sorts of excuses not to deal with the reality of Jesus's authority.

Let Jesus tell you what to do about alcohol, pornography, and your speech, heart, relationships, future, hope, and faith. Let His rule overrule your flesh, and you will be set free.

———

Jesus, *take charge. Give me a heart to obey Your commands and to serve Your kingdom in all that I do. I am so honored to be in Your presence and to be one of Your heirs. Amen.*

Citizens of Heaven

Our citizenship is in heaven, from which also we eagerly
wait for a Savior, the Lord Jesus Christ.

PHILIPPIANS 3:20

If you travel abroad, you have a passport allowing you to leave the realm of your national citizenship and enter into another nation. The passport identifies you and defines you with regard to your citizenship, so much so that the governing rules of your home nation will apply to you within your nation's embassy—no matter what country you're in.

As a citizen of heaven, Jesus doesn't expect you to leave your passport at home. When you go to work, hang out with friends, or post online, you're part of God's kingdom, and Jesus wants you to represent the kingdom wherever you roam.

A lot of Christians would prefer dual citizenship, but it doesn't work that way. When we live outside Jesus's kingdom mandates, we lose access to His kingdom authority operating on our behalf. Since all authority belongs to Him, don't you think it would be wise to obey Him? He holds the authority to reverse whatever challenge you're facing. He holds the authority to overcome those coworkers seeking to bring you down. He holds the authority to turn around your financial mess, restore your marriage, or lead you in fulfilling your destiny. He's in charge—of everything. Even your trials. Even your enemies, including the greatest enemy of all time, Satan himself.

No human being has the last word over you, because no human being is the King of kings. They may be *a* king, but they are not *the* King. They may be *a* boss, but they are not *the* boss. Jesus isn't only the nice, meek babe in the manger we know Him to be. He's powerful and authoritative, and He will win any war you turn over to Him. He's your general, chief, warrior, combatant, and most importantly, King.

———

Jesus, my King, help me see where I've given authority to and surrendered to people instead of to You. I want my citizenship to be in Your kingdom only. Amen.

EXPERIENCE *the King*

FOCUS SCRIPTURE

Rejoice greatly, O daughter of Zion! Shout in triumph, O daughter of Jerusalem! Behold, your king is coming to you; He is just and endowed with salvation, humble, and mounted on a donkey (Zechariah 9:9).

Do you think you would have recognized Jesus as Lord, Savior, and King if you had witnessed Him arriving in Jerusalem on a donkey? Would you have rejoiced in His arrival? Why or why not?

_____

_____

_____

FOR REFLECTION

Describe a time you encountered Jesus as King.

_____

_____

_____

Which characteristic of the King draws you closer to Jesus? Why?

_____

_____

_____

Which message from the devotions this week did you most need—and why?

_____

_____

_____

PERSONAL PRAYER

I praise You, King, for…

_____

_____

_____

Forgive me, King, when I…

_____

_____

_____

I'm grateful to You, my King, for…

_____

_____

_____

King, today I need Your help to…

_____

_____

_____

The references to the King and His kingdom in the book of Matthew are plentiful. The magi came to worship Him after His birth, claiming that He was born King of the Jews (2:2). When John the Baptist announced the King's arrival, he said, "Repent, for the kingdom of heaven is at hand" (3:2). When Jesus was ready to reveal His kingship, He told His disciples to get Him a donkey, since it had been prophesied that the divine King would ride on one. Furthermore, as Jesus sent His disciples to preach, He told them to proclaim that the kingdom of God had arrived (10:7).

Accepting the Gift

> Every priest stands daily ministering and offering time after time the
> same sacrifices, which can never take away sins; but He, having offered
> one sacrifice for sins for all time, sat down at the right hand of God...For
> by one offering He has perfected for all time those who are sanctified.

HEBREWS 10:11-12, 14

When Adam and Eve first sinned in the garden, they tried to fix the problem by wearing fig leaves. They thought if they weren't naked, the Lord wouldn't see their shame. We may laugh a bit at that, but how many of us have tried to hide our sin rather than take it to God?

When God saw their attempt, He chose to slay an animal, shedding its blood to provide a covering for Adam and Eve that He would accept (Genesis 3:7, 21). This act led to the system of animal sacrifices we read about throughout the Old Testament by which the wrath of God could be temporarily assuaged and His creation could be reconciled to Him. Passover (Exodus 12) is one of the most well-known displays of this practice. But this initial system required ongoing sacrifices. God's people needed an ultimate sacrifice. Perfect. Human. And like them.

Jesus.

The great news of the gospel is that our sin debt has been paid in full. God allowed a permanent sacrifice—the Lamb of God—to substitute for the punishment each of us deserves. On the cross, Jesus Christ bore every sin of every person—for all time. Friend, we can all cry "Amen" to the fact that when we sin, we don't have to go searching for a quality animal sacrifice to meet Old Testament requirements. We do, however, have to accept the sacrifice of the Lamb of God. John 3:16 tells us, "God so loved the world, that He gave His only begotten Son, that whoever believes in Him shall not perish, but have eternal life." There is no life without the sacrifice. There's also no life without the acceptance of that gift.

Don't miss the most important gift ever offered. That is a sacrifice too great.

Jesus, I'm so grateful I don't have to cover up in shame because You, as the Lamb of God, were the ultimate sacrifice to reconcile me with God for eternity. Thank You. Amen.

Confidence in Christ

The next day [John the Baptist] saw Jesus coming to him and said,
"Behold, the Lamb of God who takes away the sin of the world!"

JOHN 1:29

Two brothers were playing when a bee stung the older one on the eyelid. He put his hands to his face and fell to the ground in pain. As the younger brother looked on in horror, the bee began buzzing around his head. Terrified, he screamed, "The bee's going to get me!" The older brother, regaining his composure, said, "What are you talking about? That bee can't hurt you. He's already stung me."

This is what happened on Calvary. God loves you so much that He stepped out of heaven in the person of Jesus Christ and took the "stinger of death" in your place. Jesus hung on the cross not for His own sin but for yours and mine.

How do we know that Jesus's death on the cross really took care of the sin problem? Because when Mary Magdalene came to Jesus's tomb that Sunday morning, she couldn't find Him. She saw someone she thought was a gardener and asked the man where the Lord's body had been taken. When the gardener said her name, Mary gasped in amazement. It was Jesus (John 20:1-18).

Our faith would be empty and useless if not for the resurrection. As the apostle Paul said, if Jesus were not raised, we should be the most pitied people on earth (1 Corinthians 15:16-19). But the fact is, the Lamb of God *has* been raised.

If you're counting on anything beyond Jesus for your salvation, then you're really saying Jesus Christ isn't enough. You might say, "But my mom was a Christian, and she prayed for me." Praise God. But what about you? Salvation has nothing to do with your heritage or the name of your church. It has to do with whether you've placed absolute confidence in the person and work of Christ, the Lamb of God.

———

Jesus, *if Your tomb hadn't been empty, my faith would be. Your sacrifice and Your power over death fill me with confidence and gratitude. Thank You. Amen.*

Saved for Eternity, Healed Today

He Himself bore our sins in His body on the cross, so that we might die
to sin and live to righteousness; for by His wounds you were healed.

1 PETER 2:24

Have you ever received a gift so special that your first thought was *How will I ever respond in kind?* When you truly understand this name of Jesus and what He accomplished and gifted you as the Lamb, it summons the same question. How *should* we respond to such a gift?

Live righteously.

Simple...but not easy. God, however, even took care of that burden. The Lamb of God was sacrificed so that you and I could live in spiritual victory, not spiritual defeat. He died and was resurrected so the devil would no longer own us. See, Jesus's sacrifice on the cross wasn't made just so sinners would become saints; it was also made so saints would get healed. By His stripes we are healed from addictions, fear, worry, relational issues, doubt, and much more.

Perhaps you still struggle with wounds from the past. But what the Lamb of God secured is a redemption so powerful that He can heal all the wounds you still have. I love Revelation 12:11, where it says, "They overcame [the accuser] because of the blood of the Lamb and because of the word of their testimony." Notice it doesn't say they overcame by the power of positive thinking or financial might. They overcame by the blood of the Lamb. This is because on the cross, Jesus not only paid for your sins but also broke the authority of Satan.

This truth of this name of Jesus is so important that it ought to be what you go to first when troubles come your way. Every morning declare to yourself and to the devil the truth that the Lamb of God has dealt with all your sin. Because, friend, the Lamb of God didn't just save us for eternity; He saved us for right now.

———

Jesus, I come to You with all of my wounds and ask for healing. You have saved me from them through Your own wounds, Your sacrifice. Help me be righteous in all that I do. Amen.

Worthy of Worship

He made Him who knew no sin to be sin on our behalf,
so that we might become the righteousness of God in Him.

2 CORINTHIANS 5:21

It's challenging to envision how Jesus can embody the qualities of both a lamb and a king. But once you get to the know the Lamb of God as He is to be fully known through Scripture, you come to see that the Lamb is actually a fierce and mighty King. In fact, the Lamb is the name to which you should appeal when you wage your most difficult wars.

I recently filmed a Bible study in Jackson Hole, Wyoming, a region full of some of our nation's finest examples of nature and wildlife. As we traveled throughout the various parts of this sanctuary, I noticed many signs reminding people to carry bear spray. The threat of oncoming wild bears can turn deadly if one isn't prepared to ward them off.

Similarly, the blood of the Lamb is our repellent for Satan. When Satan starts to mess with you in your home, on your job, or in your emotions and thoughts, you need to worship the Lamb of God. In doing so, you're overcoming Satan with the all-powerful blood of the Lamb that will gain you victory—not only for eternity but also for every single moment of your life.

Satan is a strong enemy. He has claws. His jaws can crush you. He's deceptive and comes at you through a variety of attempts to take you off track from living out your kingdom destiny for God. Only when you activate the power of Jesus's blood as your covering and spiritual weaponry will you walk in victory.

Understand this name. Worship this name. Apply this name. Honor this name. In this name you will find protection, power, and strength. Worthy is the Lamb.

———

Jesus, You are the mighty Lamb. You have the power to give me victory over my battles and weaknesses. I bow down and worship You. Worthy is the Lamb of God. Amen

EXPERIENCE *the Lamb of God*

FOCUS SCRIPTURE

The next day John was standing with two of his disciples, and he looked at Jesus as He walked, and said, "Behold, the Lamb of God!" The two disciples heard him speak, and they followed Jesus (John 1:35-37).

How has your life changed since you declared Jesus as the Lamb of God and started following Him?

_____

_____

_____

FOR REFLECTION

Describe a time you encountered Jesus as the Lamb.

_____

_____

_____

Which characteristic of the Lamb draws you closer to God? Why?

_____

_____

_____

Which message from the devotions this week did you most need—and why?

_____

_____

_____

PERSONAL PRAYER

I praise You, Lamb of God, for…

_____

_____

_____

Forgive me, Lamb of God, when I…

_____

_____

_____

I'm grateful to You, Lamb of God, for…

_____

_____

_____

Lamb of God, today I need Your help to…

_____

_____

_____

Jesus is called by this name more than 20 times in the book of Revelation. This final book of Scripture, which holds the mystery of God's coming kingdom, references Jesus as the Lamb over and over and over again. The slain Lamb is the only one able to open the book of judgment.

Never Give Up

Since we have a great high priest who has passed through the heavens, Jesus, the Son of God, let us hold fast our confession...let us draw near with confidence to the throne of grace, so that we may receive mercy and find grace to help in time of need.

HEBREWS 4:14, 16

You will encounter Jesus as the Great High Priest in Hebrews, which is considered one of the more challenging books of the Bible to comprehend. So allow me to start with a simple summary of its message: Never give up.

It's a message needed at the time, and it surely is a message needed today.

This book was written to a group of believers who were severely struggling with thoughts of throwing in the towel. They were tempted to walk away from the faith. They were tempted to give up or give in because life had become too hard. Living as a Christian in their culture had become too difficult. Daily, they faced persecution, challenges, and overwhelming odds. Which is why the author of Hebrews sought to remind them not to quit. Not to give in. Not to give up. Not to let their hearts, which had already grown weary, simply stop.

You might be able to identify with the audience of Hebrews. You might find yourself in a dire situation and feel tempted to quit. It could be you're raising the question *Why go on?* You feel that things will never change. It simply isn't going to get any better. You may think you'll never find the victory you're looking for or discover the life you hope to live.

Let's be honest. Even though we're Christians, go to church, say our prayers, and seek the Lord, sometimes we all feel tempted to give up. Sometimes we're merely holding on by a thread and feeling as if one small thing could tip us over.

But the author of the book of Hebrews seeks to explain why you don't have to give up or give in. And it all hinges on one name of Jesus, the one we'll explore together: Great High Priest.

———

Jesus, I will never give up. Life is hard, but the only giving in I want to do is to Your will, grace, help, and truth. Show me how to press on in faith, Lord. Amen.

He Knows Your Suffering

Christ did not glorify Himself so as to become a high priest,
but He who said to Him, "You are My Son, today I have
begotten You"; just as He says also in another passage, "You
are a priest forever according to the order of Melchizedek."

HEBREWS 5:5-6

To understand the significance of the name Great High Priest, you first need to understand the nature of the Judaic priesthood. A priest had to be taken from men and appointed on behalf of men. In other words, a priest had to be equal to those he was serving in this role. The author of Hebrews goes on to say that the priest also had to be appointed by God. A person couldn't just wake up one morning and decide he wanted to be a priest.

In addition, the priest had to offer sacrifices for sins. He had to do this for his own sin as well as for the sins of those he represented. And while these sacrifices didn't remove sin or its consequences, they did allow for a delay until the true sacrifice—Jesus—would one day come.

A priest had to have another qualification, revealed to us in Hebrews 5:2: "He can deal gently with the ignorant and misguided, since he himself also is beset with weakness." Essentially, the priest had to understand what it means to struggle. He couldn't be someone who didn't know how to have compassion for those who need it the most.

All these things give us a better concept of what it means for Jesus to be our Great High Priest. He had to qualify just like the previous priests had to qualify. He was appointed by God. He was human. He had to know and understand suffering—to weep as we weep and to comprehend what it means to struggle. In His humanity, He identified with anguish, agony, pain, emptiness, and more. Just like you and I do. Jesus, our Great High Priest, not only knows what it is to struggle and suffer but is our priest, comforter, and redeemer when we struggle and suffer.

Jesus, You know deep suffering and the hardship of humanity. What a gift that I can come to You and receive the comfort and guidance only You can bring Your children. Amen.

A Blessing of Refreshment

Melchizedek king of Salem brought out bread and wine;
now he was a priest of God Most High.

GENESIS 14:18

Jesus's lineage of priesthood was rooted in the process, programming, and historical line of Melchizedek. Now, it's easy to tune out when someone brings up a name like Melchizedek. The author of Hebrews actually explains that this happens when people become "dull of hearing." But our spiritual hearing is sharpened because we met Melchizedek when we studied the name *El Elyon*. (I encourage you to revisit those devotions or read Genesis 14 in full.)

Melchizedek is the king of Salem. During Old Testament times, Salem was a name for Jerusalem, and it means "peace." Thus, the king of Salem is the king of peace. And he is a priest. A prophet brought the Word of God to men, but a priest brought the sins of the people to God and offered up sacrifices on their behalf. We know Jesus is a prophet because He's called the Word of God (John 1). We also know He is both a priest and a king—just like Melchizedek.

A post-battle scene introduces us to Melchizedek (Genesis 14). Abram was victorious and exhausted after the war, and Melchizedek brought him wine and bread to refresh him. These offerings became a blessing. (If you'll recall, Melchizedek also honored God for the victory, unlike other kings who wanted the credit.)

Jesus came in the order of Melchizedek, and through the wine and bread of communion today, you can overcome and be refreshed from yesterday's battles as well as prepare for tomorrow's battles. It's designed to give you a fresh blessing. Jesus, your Great High Priest, has come to restore your spirit, give you strength, and provide you with a blessing in between the challenges and trials life brings.

Jesus, Your presence throughout Scripture helps me understand Your character and blessings. I come to You today for refreshment so I can face my battles and glorify Your name. Amen.

Your Anchor and Access

This hope we have as an anchor of the soul, a hope both sure
and steadfast and one which enters within the veil, where
Jesus has entered as a forerunner for us, having become a high
priest forever according to the order of Melchizedek.

HEBREWS 6:19-20

Jesus is the anchor for the soul. What does a dropped anchor do? It holds a boat steady despite how windy or stormy it might be. Even though the boat may be rocking, it never leaves its location because the anchor holds.

You need to recognize this concept: If you don't drop the anchor, it does you no good. If you don't allow Jesus as the Great High Priest to be present in your life as an anchor, the storms of life will carry you away. If you turn to Him and let Him steady you along the way, when there's turbulence at home, at your job, or in the life areas of relationships, physical and emotional well-being, or finances, you'll have an anchor. Jesus will hold you steady. He will give you hope.

Hope is not concerned with where you are right now. Hope looks to where things will wind up. Hope is joyful expectation about the future. The high priesthood of Jesus Christ holds you steady while you wait with expectation in the midst of chaos.

Not only does Jesus bring refreshment, blessing, stability, and hope, but He gives us a greater intimacy with God by taking us behind the veil. See, a priest had to pass through three areas in the tabernacle: the outer court, the Holy Place, and the Holy of Holies, where God's presence was. But Jesus Christ, by virtue of His death, burial, and resurrection, has removed the veil that divides us from God the Father.

Friend, our money won't get us there. Our status or business title won't get us there. And our efforts to earn entrance won't get us there. Only our right relationship with Jesus, the Great High Priest, gives us access to the presence of God.

———

Jesus, I praise You! You revive my spirit when I am weary. You lead me to the presence of God. And as the Great High Priest, You anchor my soul in the storms. Amen.

EXPERIENCE *the Great High Priest*

FOCUS VERSES

Although He was a Son, He learned obedience from the things which He suffered. And having been made perfect, He became to all those who obey Him the source of eternal salvation, being designated by God as a high priest according to the order of Melchizedek (Hebrews 5:8-10).

How does viewing Jesus as the Great High Priest who intimately knows suffering impact how you feel when you approach Him for His mercy and grace?

_____

_____

_____

FOR REFLECTION

Describe a time you encountered Jesus as the Great High Priest.

_____

_____

_____

Which characteristic of the Great High Priest draws you closer to God? Why?

_____

_____

_____

Which message from the devotions this week did you most need—and why?

_____

_____

_____

PERSONAL PRAYER

I praise You, Great High Priest, for…

_____

_____

_____

Forgive me, Great High Priest, when I…

_____

_____

_____

I'm grateful to You, Great High Priest, for…

_____

_____

_____

Great High Priest, today I need Your help to…

_____

_____

_____

Jesus didn't pass through the three areas of the tabernacle for us as the human priests did. Instead, He passed through the three levels of the heavens. When He died and then rose from the grave, He ascended on a cloud and passed through the atmospheric heavens, the stellular heavens, and then into what is known as the third heavens—the throne room of God. He passed through the heavens in order to be seated on the throne at the right hand of the Father.

He Carries Us All

A child will be born to us, a son will be given to us; and the government
will rest on His shoulders: and His name will be called Wonderful
Counselor, Mighty God, Eternal Father, Prince of Peace.

ISAIAH 9:6

There's a story about a wicked storm in the Midwest. As people scrambled for shelter, a man saw a boy carrying another boy about his size on his back. The man shouted, "That boy looks heavy. Do you need help?"

To which the boy doing the carrying replied, "Oh, he's not heavy; he's my brother."

When the weight of a loved one is on our shoulders, love itself gives us the strength to carry them. That same love is found in Jesus. But Jesus doesn't carry only one of us on His back; He carries all of us. Which is why the name Sovereign is so important. It gives us a glimpse into just how much God is for us—for *you*.

According to the prophet Isaiah, the Christ child would carry the weight of the government on His shoulders. Only one entity carries the weight of the government on its shoulders, and that entity is known as a sovereign. While one day Jesus will physically return to the earth and set up His rule in Jerusalem to govern the whole world from Israel, He currently holds the position of spiritual ruler over His people, His church—the citizens of His kingdom. Not only does He oversee us, but He carries us on His shoulders.

When we allow Jesus to govern us, He carries the weight of all that needs to be maneuvered and accomplished. He does so with tenderness, wisdom, and authority. As we explore the roles and attributes of Jesus listed in today's verse, may you find yourself trusting the strength and love of Jesus as Sovereign to carry you through any storm and through all of life.

———

Jesus, *as the kingdom leader, You could rule with anger and force. But You choose love and wisdom. I am grateful for Your grace-filled governing. Amen.*

Wonderful Counselor

Trust in the LORD with all your heart and do not lean on
your own understanding. In all your ways acknowledge
Him, and He will make your paths straight.

PROVERBS 3:5-6

The first governing position Isaiah shares with us in this series of descriptions is that of a counselor. One of the reasons life gets so distorted for us is that we lean too much on our own counsel and understanding—or we look for too many other people to give us advice. We get pulled in many directions and lose sight of our path and God's truth.

This doesn't happen when we first seek Jesus the Wonderful Counselor. The guidance, direction, insight, and clarity He provides is always accurate, timely, and helpful. Jesus doesn't merely possess perfect knowledge; He also possesses perfect understanding.

Sovereign knows not only the path you've been on and the one you should take, but also the emotional and mental roadblocks preventing you from overcoming what you face or reaching your goal—and how to address them. In short, He can both guide and empathize.

He owns the corner on counsel because He knows the end from the beginning, down from up, and everything in between. But there are conditions for obtaining His counsel. We find three of them in John 7:17, Ecclesiastes 2:26, and Proverbs 1:7: doing God's will, being good in His sight, and fearing Him.

All of that can be summed up in one word: *alignment.* When you align your heart, mind, thoughts, words, and decisions under the overarching Sovereign and His rule in your life, you gain access to His wisdom and knowledge. In every moment, every circumstance, He gets it. He gets you. And He's ready to guide your steps, your heart, and your path through the twists and turns of life as you align with His truth and way.

———

Jesus, may I do Your will, be good in Your sight, and fear You. Sovereign, I want to be aligned under You and acknowledge You in every part of my life. Amen.

Mighty God

I will come with the mighty deeds of the Lord GOD;
I will make mention of Your righteousness, Yours alone.

PSALM 71:16

Not only will Jesus your Sovereign give you perfect advice as your Wonderful Counselor, but He also has the power to see things through to completion in whatever way He directs you because He is the Mighty God.

When you take your car to the dealership, it's because you don't have what's needed to resolve the blinking light or the irritating noise. The mechanics, however, can run the diagnostics and make use of their knowledge, tools, and experience to go from identifying the problem to implementing the solution.

If you go to Jesus for His wonderful counsel and allow Him to perform His diagnostics, He has all the tools, power, and might to deliver you. His peace will calm your chaos. His skills can rectify any confusion. His healing can mend your relationships and brokenness. See, the Mighty God is so powerful that He requires nothing outside Himself to restore everything that needs to be restored in your life.

You may feel like you have the strength or know-how to navigate a trial or two, but when they pile up as they tend to do, you need the power source of Jesus your Sovereign. Throughout the Gospels we see the power of this descriptive name manifested. One example is His strength over sin. He demonstrated His ability to forgive sin and redeem people from the consequences they faced, and then He urged them to go and sin no more. He also drove out demons. Healed the sick. Raised the dead.

Friend, Jesus has the authority to overrule anything you need Him to—whether physical, emotional, or spiritual. He is the Mighty God, the divine Sovereign, the one to approach even before the warning lights blink. He is the one to praise and credit in the process and when you're back up and running smoothly again.

———

Jesus, *I come to You for diagnosis, help, healing, guidance, and restoration. You rule over my sins and struggles. I depend on and declare Your power and might, Lord. Amen.*

Eternal Father and Prince of Peace

I have told you these things so that in Me you may have peace. You will have suffering in this world. Be courageous! I have conquered the world.

JOHN 16:33 HCSB

The story is told of a flight that hit major turbulence during a thunderstorm. As the plane was tossed side to side, passengers shrieked and screamed. That is, except for one small boy. He sat calmly as he drew a picture of himself climbing a tree on a sunny day. No one ever would have guessed he was on the same plane as the others.

A lady nearby noticed his calmness and asked, "Why aren't you afraid?"

He just looked up, smiled, and said, "Because my dad is the pilot."

Sometimes life is frightening and seemingly destined for a crash. But knowing that the Eternal Father and Prince of Peace sits at the controls ought to eliminate the drama and fill us with peace.

In Israel, you hear *Shalom* used as a greeting. It's a pregnant word, containing much more than our contemporary understanding of the term *peace*. The concept of *shalom* is wellness or being well ordered. So when a Jewish person says "Shalom," they're saying they hope your life is put together in order. Our Eternal Father, outside of time and our human limits, can command even our biggest storms. And as the Prince of Peace, our Sovereign can usher peace into our most painful chaos. But we must surrender to and align with Jesus as the only true source. He stated this clearly in the verse featured today. We may seek this peace in other places, but we won't find it in other sources. Only Jesus has conquered what brings us angst or unrest.

If thunder and lightning are tossing you about, you can be at peace. You know the pilot—the true Sovereign—Wonderful Counselor, Mighty God, Eternal Father, and Prince of Peace. In Him, you find counsel, power, direction, and peace. In Him you find everything you need.

———

Jesus, *I can rest in the storm. When change or worry brew around me, I don't have to assume the crash position, because I know You as Sovereign. Amen.*

EXPERIENCE *the Sovereign*

FOCUS SCRIPTURE

For by Him all things were created, both in the heavens and on earth, visible and invisible, whether thrones or dominions or rulers or authorities—all things have been created through Him and for Him (Colossians 1:16).

The world was created through and for Jesus. How are you depending on the power of Sovereign for your family, job, counsel, troubles, peace?

_____

_____

_____

FOR REFLECTION

Describe a time you encountered Jesus as Sovereign.

_____

_____

_____

Which characteristic of Sovereign draws you closer to God? Why?

_____

_____

_____

Which message from the devotions this week did you most need—and why?

_____

_____

_____

PERSONAL PRAYER

I praise You, Sovereign, for…

_____

_____

_____

Forgive me, Sovereign, when I…

_____

_____

_____

I'm grateful to You, Sovereign, for…

_____

_____

_____

Sovereign, today I need Your help to…

_____

_____

_____

We uncover the concept of this name in the pages of an Old Testament passage—Isaiah 9:6—which is just as applicable now as it was when it was penned. It would be almost seven hundred years before the incarnation of this prophetic name would come about. It would be a long haul of difficulties, trials, and dangers for the Israelites until God became flesh and Jesus, Sovereign, would be born.

Everything You Need

Jesus said to them, "Truly, truly, I say to you,
before Abraham was born, I am."

JOHN 8:58

Jesus is God's selfie. Why? Because a selfie reflects the image of the person taking the photo. And without Jesus, we cannot see and intimately know God's heart, His person, or His character because He is wholly other and sits outside our realm of understanding.

Out of God's great love for us, He desired to be known and seen by us. So in order to do that, He had to come to us in a form we would be able to understand. He had to be both man and God simultaneously.

In the book of John, we come across my favorite name of Jesus: I Am. This is a name you can't embrace halfway. Either Jesus is I Am, or He's a liar. That sounds harsh, but even Jesus said He would be a liar if He claimed not to know the Father (John 8:55).

He took this name—the same name God presented as His own (I Am, YHWH)—when He sought to explain who He was in relationship to mankind. By examining the name I Am, we get a closer look at the heart of God. It's a personal pronoun, and it's present tense. He exists in the eternal present tense, and only one being can claim that: God Himself.

Friend, when you know I Am, you will experience the full manifestation of His power and presence both in and through you. When you humble yourself under this great name, you will discover the amazing plans He has for you and the power He has for you to carry out those plans.

I don't know what challenge you might be facing, but I do know this: I Am is everything you need. Know Him more fully, seek Him more passionately, and align yourself under Him more intentionally to access the power of this personal name.

Jesus, You are the essence, flesh, and face of God. And You are everything I need. Thank You for showing me the heart of the Creator. Amen.

Bread of Life and the Light

I am the bread of life; he who comes to Me will not hunger, and he who believes in Me will never thirst...I am the Light of the world; he who follows Me will not walk in the darkness, but will have the Light of life.

JOHN 6:35; 8:12

When we're worried about whether we'll have enough of what we need or find ourselves in a dark season where we struggle to find our footing, we're seeking the provision and the light of I Am.

The Israelites found themselves in this situation. They were wandering the desolate wilderness and needed sustenance. So God sent down bread from heaven called manna. In the middle of nowhere, He provided all they needed for survival. As I Am and the bread of life, He does the same for us.

Not only does Jesus feed our spirits, but He illuminates us. When we follow Him, He allows us to see where we're going. The proof that many of us don't know this name or apply its power in our lives is that we keep seeking nourishment from sources that aren't life-giving, going down wrong paths, and making wrong decisions. But Jesus says when we come to know Him in a close, abiding manner, He gives us light for our path and supplies wisdom. He blesses us with provision even in the most desolate times.

Many defeats, addictions, and relational crises occur today because our souls are unnecessarily starved and our lives are lived in darkness. Matthew 5:6 tells us there's only one way to be satisfied: "Blessed are those who hunger and thirst for righteousness, for they shall be satisfied."

Only Jesus can satiate our hunger and quench our thirst. Only Jesus, I Am, can bring clarity to the spiritually blind. And only you can decide whether you will be among the blessed who hunger for righteousness and seek it by believing in and following I Am. This is the way to light, life, and satisfaction that leaves you wanting for nothing.

———

Jesus, the ways You provide are endless. When I'm grumbling, I need to remember that You are the bread of life and the sustenance I need to carry on. I hunger for You alone. Amen.

Your Door and Your Shepherd

Truly, truly, I say to you, I am the door of the sheep...
I am the good shepherd; the good shepherd
lays down His life for the sheep.

JOHN 10:7, 11

Friend, you are to have super-life. And the way you obtain super-life is by abiding in the name of Jesus. When you realize that He not only illuminates the pathways of life but also grants access to those pathways as the door, you will come to understand He is all and over all.

This "I Am" offers entrance. Every shepherd has a gate through which the sheep can enter. In John 10:9, Jesus says, "I am the door; if anyone enters through Me, he will be saved, and will go in and out and find pasture." This door grants us entrance into heaven. And through this door we also discover freedom and good pasture here on earth. Though many of us have tried, we can't go around Jesus to get to good pasture. If we want to make our way to a place of deep satisfaction, we must go through the door, through Jesus. It's no surprise that the name translated "Lord" in the well-known and loved Psalm 23 reference "The Lord is my shepherd" is the name we're looking at here: YHWH. I Am.

When Jesus is our shepherd, He takes care of our directional needs, leading us in the paths of righteousness. He takes care of our spiritual well-being, causing us to lie down in green pastures. He takes care of our emotional needs, helping us fear no evil. He also takes care of our eternal needs, having goodness and mercy follow us all the days of our life and allowing us to ultimately dwell in the house of the Lord forever.

As the great I Am, Jesus has your back directionally, spiritually, emotionally, physically, and eternally. Enter the gate and walk into His pasture. Let I Am care for you.

———

Jesus, You are the doorway to deep satisfaction and freedom. I enter into the peaceful pastures where You care for me and guide my steps today and throughout eternity. Amen.

The Way, the Truth, and the Life

I am the resurrection and the life; he who believes in Me
will live even if he dies...I am the way, and the truth, and
the life; no one comes to the Father but through Me.

JOHN 11:25; 14:6

Jesus came that He might give life, but He also came as the life itself. He is the power of resurrection, and He is life. When you allow life's troubles and trials to drive you to Him, you will experience His power not only to calm you in the chaos but to also resurrect those things in your life you thought were dead.

Most of us go through our lives hoping we know where we're going. We seek and search and ask people we encounter. But Jesus didn't just tell us He knows the way; He told us He *is* the way. He's both our personal GPS and the destination. When we abide in Him and align ourselves under Him, He takes us where we need to go. He opens those doors we didn't even have the ability to knock on. He removes those people who sought to remove us first. He overcomes the obstacles our emotions may throw in our path.

Not only that, but Jesus is the truth. Now, I didn't say He's *a* truth. He's *the* truth. I Am provides an absolute standard by which all else is measured. There's an absolute standard for the definition of the beginning of life and for marriage. There's an absolute standard for addressing racial issues, helping the poor, and serving others. Jesus is the standard, and He has spoken. The only way to access the life He died to give you here on earth—the abundant life—is to follow His path according to His truth.

When we believe I Am and come to God through Him, we can look to Him as *the* way for career, family, hopes, destiny, healing, faith, provision, and purpose. We can have life even when we die.

———

Jesus, You are the truth, the standard. As I Am, You remove obstacles in my path so I can press on. I don't need an alternate route. You are the way, and I am following. Amen.

EXPERIENCE *the I Am*

FOCUS SCRIPTURE

Jesus, knowing all the things that were coming upon Him, went forth and said to them, "Whom do you seek?" They answered Him, "Jesus the Nazarene." He said to them, "I am He." And Judas also, who was betraying Him, was standing with them. So when He said to them, "I am He," they drew back and fell to the ground (John 18:4-6).

What do you learn about Jesus from this moment in Scripture?

_____

_____

_____

FOR REFLECTION

Describe a time you encountered Jesus as I Am.

_____

_____

_____

Which characteristic of I Am draws you closer to God? Why?

_____

_____

_____

Which message from the devotions this week did you most need—and why?

_____

_____

_____

PERSONAL PRAYER

I praise You, I Am, for...

_____

_____

_____

Forgive me, I Am, when I...

_____

_____

_____

I'm grateful to You, I Am, for...

_____

_____

_____

I Am, today I need Your help to...

_____

_____

_____

The name I Am is called the *tetragrammaton*, which means "the four letters." I Am comprises four consonants in the Hebrew language. Originally, the Hebrew language was written in abjad (a form of symbolic writing), meaning it had no vowels. This name of God has no vowels, so it couldn't be pronounced exactly as written. In order to talk about God, one must insert vowels into the name YHWH.

Power Versus Authority

He put all things in subjection under His feet, and gave
Him as head over all things to the church, which is His
body, the fullness of Him who fills all in all.

EPHESIANS 1:22-23

The name Lord isn't just something to throw into prayers to make our offerings sound more spiritual or make ourselves sound holy. This name carries much more than semantic illusions. It carries authority. Yet when seeking connection with the Lord, there's a good chance most of us have experienced interference.

When we don't know this name or how to relate to it while on earth, we experience an interruption in the signal. The enemy has been allowed power to disrupt the communication and alignment we have with Jesus.

But let's not confuse the terms *power* and *authority*. Satan has power to dominate the world in which we live and influence people's lives in countless ways. His tactics and destruction are both real and damaging. But what he doesn't have is final authority. Authority is the right to use the power you possess. God has given His Son ultimate authority over what happens in history. He's placed all things in subjection to Him.

Let's go to the football field for a minute. Football players are generally bigger and stronger than the referees. The referees are often older, smaller, and more out of shape than the players. The players can knock someone down. They can even interfere with and disrupt the other team's best plays. That's called power. But the referees can put someone out of a game. That's called authority.

See, Satan has power, but the only way he's free to use that power over you is through your failure to operate in alignment with Jesus as Lord. When you're under the covering of the lordship of Christ, you stand protected. No one can knock you down. And no one can pull you from the game.

———

Jesus, when I get lost in worries about everyday things, I'm forgetting whom I worship. I'm forgetting about Your power and authority. Forgive me, mighty Lord. Amen.

Which Kingdom Do You Serve?

He rescued us from the domain of darkness,
and transferred us to the kingdom of His beloved Son.

COLOSSIANS 1:13

As believers, we used to belong to Satan's kingdom and rulership before meeting the Lord. But God rescued us from the authority of darkness and out of the wrong kingdom so we could live our lives under the rule of a new King, the Lord Jesus Christ. This also means that for Satan to have power over our lives and the institutions of kingdom followers, he has to get us to leave the Lord's kingdom rule and come back over to his.

Your response might be, "I would never choose Satan's kingdom!" But when we aren't attentive and aligned with the Lord, the lines between the two kingdoms blur. Much of this happens through the division of the secular and the sacred when people participate in church under one kingdom, then go out into the world on Monday and function under the influence of another kingdom. We create this flip-flop of kingdoms and then wonder why there's not more victory in our life.

We are not helpless, my friend. Since Satan can't rule our lives with any rightful authority, we have the choice and free will to yield to the Lord instead. When we align with the Lord and honor His headship, we access His sovereign authority over all things, including our thoughts, choices, words, and perspective.

Give the Lord His proper place in your life, home, and church. Ask Him to reveal the blurred lines you've knowingly or unknowingly crossed that are keeping you from residing full-time in the Lord's kingdom. And even before that, bow to the Lord, surrender all to His authority, and stake your eternal residence in His kingdom.

———

Jesus, I look back at the times I've chosen a way, word, or path of the wrong kingdom. I pray to honor Your headship with my head, heart, and spirit. Amen.

Start Confessing

Many even of the rulers believed in Him, but because of
the Pharisees they were not confessing Him, for fear that
they would be put out of the synagogue; for they loved the
approval of men rather than the approval of God.

JOHN 12:42-43

Friend, if you're embarrassed to have any public association with Jesus as Lord, then you're sabotaging your own spiritual pathway to living your destiny—just like the Pharisees in today's verses. Sure, plenty of crosses hang around Christians' necks or on church walls, but for Jesus to be Lord of our lives means He rules. He chooses. There's no area of your finances, relationships, attitudes, work, or anything else that He cannot and should not overrule.

Jesus is not a decoration, a logo, or a brand. He is Lord. Ruler. Master. King. Until this lordship question is settled both in and through you publicly, heaven's help and Jesus's divine presence, intervention, transformation, deliverance, healing, and guidance will elude you simply because you do not confess Him as Lord.

Many people of today's church don't live victorious lives because, like the Pharisees, they dread the disapproval of people. They may wear T-shirts with faith slogans, but they stop short of obedience by not stating who has authority and influence over more than their wardrobe. Sadly, the failure to publicly confess Jesus as Lord blocks our ability to be delivered (saved) in our everyday life situations. John 5:23 says, "He who does not honor the Son does not honor the Father who sent Him."

Look at your life. If Jesus is prominent but not preeminent, or if He's popular, just not primary, then it's time to do more than place your faith in Christ. Scripture demands that you get to know the name Lord and confess it (publicly affirm, attest to, and identify with it). Jesus *is* your access to all you need to live your life according to the maximum expression and power you can have.

Jesus, I confess that You are my Lord, and I pray to be bold in stating this to those in my world. May my actions and words and hope honor You and the Father. Amen.

Call on Him

At the name of Jesus every knee will bow,
of those who are in heaven and on earth and under the earth,
and...every tongue will confess that Jesus Christ
is Lord, to the glory of God the Father.

PHILIPPIANS 2:10-11

A story is told about an indigenous boy who was about to be mauled by a lion. A nearby man quickly grabbed some wire and jumped on the lion's back. When he wrapped the wire around the lion's throat, the beast's attention turned from the boy to its own pain. The boy ran off while the man wrestled with the lion long enough to make his own escape.

A few weeks later, the man heard people outside his home. He looked to see what was going on and saw the young boy and some others walking up to his door. They were carrying what looked like the boy's belongings. Confused, the man asked the boy what he was doing. The boy replied, "You saved my life. And in my tribe, when someone saves your life, they own you. I am in your service for the rest of my life."

This fictional story paints a picture with which we can identify. Jesus exercised His authority and power as Lord to save us so we could pass from death to life into eternity. If you're a born-again believer, Jesus has saved your life. Yet not only does He save it for eternity, but He offers to save your life each and every moment you call on Him while publicly confessing His lordship over you.

Make a commitment that, from this moment forward, you will seek to publicly confess the name of Jesus as Lord in all you do and say. Acknowledge Him and what He's done to save you. Commit to be of His service the rest of your life. Then watch heaven pour out its unending power on you and bring heaven's intervention into your life.

———

Jesus, I bow down to You with my body and my heart. I humble myself before You and ask to be used for Your purposes now and always. Amen.

EXPERIENCE *the Lord*

FOCUS SCRIPTURE

There is no distinction between Jew and Greek; for the same Lord is Lord of all, abounding in riches for all who call on Him; for "Whoever will call on the name of the LORD will be saved" (Romans 10:12-13).

When did you call on the name of the Lord for your salvation?

_____

_____

_____

FOR REFLECTION

Describe a time you encountered Jesus as Lord.

_____

_____

_____

Which characteristic of the Lord draws you closer to God? Why?

_____

_____

_____

Which message from the devotions this week did you most need—and why?

_____

_____

_____

PERSONAL PRAYER

I praise You, Lord, for...

_____

_____

_____

Forgive me, Lord, when I...

_____

_____

_____

I'm grateful to You, Lord, for...

_____

_____

_____

Lord, today I need Your help to...

_____

_____

_____

The word *Lord* comes from the Greek word *kurios*, as used in the Septua-gint. The Septuagint is the Greek translation of the Old Testament. In the original Hebrew, *kurios* is the word *Yahweh*. Thus, when attached to Jesus, the title is a reference to His deity. When you use the name Lord to refer to Jesus, you're recognizing Him as the supreme ruler.

Our Deliverer

She will bear a Son; and you shall call His name Jesus,
for He will save His people from their sins.

MATTHEW 1:21

Do you know the story of how you were named? Our name holds special meaning for us and for those who call on us for friendship, help, or family connection. Outside of our circles, however, our name might not spark passionate responses of praise and devotion. But we know the name that does: Jesus.

The story of how Jesus got His name has to be the most amazing story in all of history. In Scripture's account of His birth, we discover that God sent a message to Joseph through an angel and told him to name the child Mary would deliver Jesus. This child was not Joseph's biological offspring, but Joseph would help raise Him. Thus, the message of what to call Jesus came to His earthly father from His heavenly Father.

At the time, Jesus was a common name, but God chose the name for an uncommon reason. The Old Testament name for Jesus was the Hebrew name Joshua. If you'll recall, Joshua was the man who delivered the Israelites into the Promised Land. He was fierce and full of faith. He led the Israelites in such a way as to overcome the enemies in the land. The name Joshua (and its corresponding Greek name, Jesus) refers to someone who leads the way into a place of blessing—a person who delivers people from their enemies.

Thus, God chose a name for His only-begotten Son that means "Savior," "rescuer," and "deliverer." The primary identity reflected in Jesus's name is that of someone who came to deliver people from something over which they needed victory. Jesus came to rescue you and me, and He calls us by name to receive that salvation and eternal life. May there be no name sweeter to your ears than Jesus.

———

Jesus, when I hear Your name, my heart softens. My human spirit responds to it with joy and gratitude. And when I face trials, I know You as my deliverer. Amen.

Mission Possible: Grace

He who believes in the Son has eternal life; but he who does not
obey the Son will not see life, but the wrath of God abides on him.

JOHN 3:36

When I was a water safety instructor and lifeguard, I had roles like teaching people how to swim and offering guidance on ways to swim better. But all of that was secondary to my primary goal and role: saving lives should anyone be at risk of drowning.

I'm emphasizing this idea of a foundational role because people often want to use Jesus for everything other than His primary role. They want Him to rescue them from poor health, debt, relationship issues, emotional issues, and more. And while Jesus is sufficient to come to our aid in all these things, if we don't first look to Him as the One who rescues us from our sins, we bypass the foundation upon which all else rests.

The central mission of Jesus is that of saving us from our sins—both saving us for eternity through His atonement and saving us on earth through His ongoing intercession, supplying us power to resist and overcome temptation and the continual consequences of sin (Hebrews 7:25).

He came to save us and give us eternal life, but He also came so we might fully experience that life in the present (John 10:10). When we go to Jesus as though He's a vending machine instead of our rescuer, however, we're denying His true power and our need for Him, His death, His resurrection, and His redemption.

I understand that most people don't want to talk about sin. In fact, they avoid it so much that they usually refer to sin as a "mistake," an "issue," a "stumble." Be the child of God who acknowledges your sin. Come forward with it, and bow down at Jesus's feet, knowing that above all else, you need the full grace of the Savior.

———

Jesus, when I neglect to bring my sin to You, I miss the chance to have Your power at work in my life. Humbly, today I come to You with my confessions to receive Your grace. Amen.

The Reality of Sin

You were washed, but you were sanctified, but you were justified in the name of the Lord Jesus Christ and in the Spirit of our God.

1 CORINTHIANS 6:11

S peaking of sinning, we've all done it. And whether it's a sin of commission (something done purposefully) or a sin of omission (not doing what should be done—James 4:17), all sin results in death. To understand our relationship to sin, let's look at the three distinct categories: imputed, inherited, and personal.

- *Imputed Sin*—The word *imputed* means "credited to someone's account." In Romans 5:12, we come across our imputed sin: "Just as through one man sin entered into the world, and death through sin, and so death spread to all men, because all sinned." The whole human race was credited with the consequence of Adam's sin: death.

- *Inherited Sin*—Inherited sin is what we receive from our parents and ancestors, and it's what we pass on to our children. We know this as our "sin nature." That's why a parent never has to teach a child how to be selfish, how to be sneaky, or how to lie. Instead, they need to teach a child to share, love, and be patient.

- *Personal Sin*—Let's forget those who came before us for a moment and just look at you and me. Personal sin is the sin we know we shouldn't do, but we go ahead and do it anyway. Some of us may let others see it more than the next person, but God doesn't look at humanity like we do; He looks at the heart (1 Samuel 16:7). Whether personal sin shows up boldly or lurks behind a veil of secrecy, God knows it's there.

This topic can be overwhelming, but we can embrace a simple truth: Sin can never be hidden; it can only be forgiven. And thanks to the authority of the name Jesus, that forgiveness can be ours.

———

Jesus, the world pretends the problem of sin isn't real, but I've experienced its damage and pain. Because of Your forgiveness, however, my problem has a solution. Amen.

In Jesus's Name

Everyone who lives and believes in Me will never die.

JOHN 11:26

Are you ready for some good news about the bad news of sin? Jesus came so we would never have to die. When you choose to abide in Him and allow His Word to abide in you, obeying Him as best you can and seeking forgiveness for when you don't, you'll discover that this name opens doors no one else could have ever opened for you.

But Jesus's name isn't a magical term like *hocus-pocus*. Rather, when it's used in conjunction with a right relationship to Him, His name gives you access to a power greater than any magic or superhero powers could ever be.

In Acts 19, we see a perfect example of this. Because Paul had traveled around casting out demons in Jesus's name, other people began to see this as a profit-producing business. They thought the secret sauce was Jesus's name, so they proceeded to use it. When they went to cast out a demon, however, the demon told them point blank that while it had heard of Paul and knew Jesus, it didn't know them. And it didn't obey them.

This truth applies to all of us as well. God will not respond to your use of Jesus's name if you aren't equally concerned with doing His will. Friend, if you're going to end your prayers with "in Jesus's name," make sure you're first letting God identify your sin in order for you to repent and receive His offer of forgiveness. Then He will address the circumstances and deliverance for which you just prayed. Why pray with a trendy tagline when you can pray in the mighty power of Jesus's name?

———

Jesus, I believe You are my Savior, Lord, and King. With the power of eternity in Your mighty name, You open doors to my hope and future. Amen.

EXPERIENCE *Jesus*

FOCUS SCRIPTURE

The sting of death is sin, and the power of sin is the law; but thanks be to God, who gives us the victory through our Lord Jesus Christ (1 Corinthians 15:56-57).

Jesus overcame death. In what way does this miracle influence how you live?

_____

_____

_____

FOR REFLECTION

Describe a time you encountered Jesus.

_____

_____

_____

Which characteristic of Jesus draws you closer to God? Why?

_____

_____

_____

Which message from the devotions this week did you most need—and why?

_____

_____

_____

PERSONAL PRAYER

I praise You, Jesus, for…

_____

_____

_____

Forgive me, Jesus, when I…

_____

_____

_____

I'm grateful to You, Jesus, for…

_____

_____

_____

Jesus, today I need Your help to…

_____

_____

_____

Jesus, a unique part of the Godhead, became a slave for us and emptied Himself. The two natures of Jesus Christ form what theologians call the *hypostatic union*—a big term that simply refers to the reality that Jesus is made up of undiminished deity and perfect humanity. He became no less God when He became human. Mary didn't give birth to both God and a man. Jesus was not 50 percent human and 50 percent God. Rather, Mary gave birth to the God-man.

Nothing Compares

I count all things to be loss in view of the surpassing value of
knowing Christ Jesus my Lord, for whom I have suffered the loss of
all things, and count them but rubbish so that I may gain Christ.

PHILIPPIANS 3:8

*T*ony Evans* is my personal identity. *Doctor* is my title. *Pastor* is my role or responsibility. *Poppy* signifies my relationship with my grandchildren. We can refer to one person in a great many ways based on the relationship and setting, and with that perspective, let's look again at some of Jesus's names.

Jesus is our Lord's personal identity. The meaning of that name is "Savior" and "deliverer." Jesus's personal name references His purpose and ability to rescue and deliver us. When the names King of kings and Lord of lords are packaged together, He is known as the Lord Jesus Christ. While all the Bible writers who referenced Him were speaking about the same person, each of His names has a unique nuance.

Christ is not Jesus's last name. It's His role or office. The word *Christ* is the Greek translation of the Hebrew word *Messiah*. That's why John 1:41 says, "[Andrew] found first his own brother Simon and said to him, 'We have found the Messiah' (which translated means Christ)."

The entire Old Testament was written in anticipation of the one to come to fulfill the role of Messiah. This is known as the messianic hope. Generation after generation looked forward to this promised person of God who would come not only for the Israelites but to impact the entire world through the establishment of the kingdom of God on earth. The person they looked for was the Messiah, known in Greek (the language of the New Testament) as the Christ.

Jesus is the Christ, the anointed one from God who fulfills the promises put forth by God for the world and for you personally. No one—and no thing—compares to Jesus the Christ. Praise the name.

———

Jesus, *You came to fulfill the role of Messiah. You sacrificed and suffered greatly so that believers can call on You. I will praise You so others might know the Christ has come. Amen.*

The Lineage of Jesus

[Andrew] found first his own brother Simon and said to him,
"We have found the Messiah" (which translated means Christ).

JOHN 1:41

Now, I know reading names and genealogies in the Bible probably isn't your favorite thing to do—nor is it mine. But those Scriptures with who begat whom are critical reading because of how they relate to prophecy and provide evidence of God's faithfulness in fulfilling His promises.

In AD 70, after the Jews' rejection of Christ, the Roman general Titus destroyed the Jewish temple as well as the city of Jerusalem. In this widespread destruction, the genealogical records for the Jews were lost. All the records except for one, that is. The record of Jesus's lineage was preserved for us in the writings of Matthew and Luke. And through this, we discover that when God connected Mary and Joseph, He connected two people who were both descended from David. The Old Testament prophecy that the Messiah would come through the Davidic line was proven. This reminds us that God knows how to bring two people together in order to fulfill His kingdom purposes. He is always intentional.

In the verse for today, Andrew said they had found the anointed one. He was referring to the anointed one who had come through the line of David. Now, in Scripture, to receive an anointing was to be elected to an office and empowered for that office. In today's culture, you could consider it akin to having an election where candidates run for a public office.

In biblical days, someone could be "elected" to one of three distinct offices. Why does the so-called politics of the time relate to the name of Christ? Because God's promise and plan was that these three classifications of anointing—that of prophet, priest, and king—were each to be fulfilled in one role at a future date through the Messiah.

Friend, God is always intentional. It's no accident that you found the Messiah. Because of His shed blood, you receive the promises and power of Christ.

—

I praise You, Christ. You are anointed as the prophet, priest, and king. God's plan for You was intentional, and I know His plan for me to follow You is intentional as well. Amen.

He Is Your Access

You have died and your life is hidden with Christ in God.

COLOSSIANS 3:3

Every time you hear or read the name Christ, you should also think of the name Messiah. And every time you hear or read the name Messiah, you should also think of the name Christ. For both of these names, you should also think of the term *anointed one*. The anointed one has been placed in this role for the benefit of each of us who believes.

Now, unfortunately, a lot of Christians relate to Christ similarly to how a lot of American citizens relate to the role of president of the United States. You'll often hear Americans say things like, "Well, he may be the president, but he's not my president." They'll say this because they didn't vote for him, or because they don't agree with his temperament or policies. Essentially, they're making it known that although he may hold the position, they won't allow that position to rule over them.

While some people may not publicly say this about Christ, they imply it with their actions. Their actions proclaim *He may be the King, but He's not king over me. He may be on the throne, but I won't let Him tell me what to do.* Christ is the anointed King, but if He's not allowed to rule in your decision-making, ideology, career, finances, and relationships, then you may be calling Him by His title without functionally allowing Him to carry out His position.

Friend, our hope is rooted in Christ, and we are hidden in Christ, accepted by Christ, and clothed in Christ. To know Christ personally and relationally is to gain access to all He embodies for us. You receive His provision, power, and blessings to the degree that you align yourself under and abide with His person. Check to see if you're clothed in Christ and are under His authority for your daily life.

———

Jesus, under Your authority, I have access to Your power and promises. The blessings that flow in my circumstances are from Your hand and from Your sacrifice. Thank You, Christ. Amen.

Live by Faith

I have been crucified with Christ; and it is no longer I who live, but
Christ lives in me; and the life which I now live in the flesh I live by
faith in the Son of God, who loved me and gave Himself up for me.

GALATIANS 2:20

Today's verse—one of my favorites—sheds light on how we experience the
goodness of Christ. Memorize this verse. Meditate on this verse. It's the key
to victory in all areas of your life. We see that what we've been crucified with is the
anointing itself. When Paul says Christ lives in us, he's referring to the anointing.
The prophet, priest, and king lives in each of us.

You are no longer to live on your own. Rather, you're now living according to
the person who carries out these three offices perfectly. Let me explain it through a
cup of coffee. My morning coffee starts out black, but then I add sugar and cream.
It's still coffee, but it's now transformed coffee. The dark is now lighter. The bitter is now sweeter.

When you and I have union with Christ personally and relationally, we're still
who we were in our original fallen state, but now we've been stirred with the person of Christ. We've added His transforming presence to us. We have everything
the three roles of prophet, priest, and king gained for us through union with Christ,
but only to the degree that we allow Christ to live in us and make His presence
known through us do we access all He has for us in these three roles.

By placing your faith in the Son of God, you give Christ permission to let His
anointing flow through you. Relying on Christ and resting in Christ for all things
is the greatest life strategy you could ever apply. Your life should flow with the
anointing of Christ. And it will when you allow Him to be your final word, your
mediating priest, and your ruler.

---

*You aren't beside me, Christ; You're in me. And this new life I live is the one
You create in Your wisdom and grace. I live by faith because You are Lord of my life. Amen.*

EXPERIENCE *Christ*

FOCUS SCRIPTURE

My goal is that they may be encouraged in heart and united in love, so that they may have the full riches of complete understanding, in order that they may know the mystery of God, namely, Christ, in whom are hidden all the treasures of wisdom and knowledge (Colossians 2:2-3 NIV).

What situation do you need to bring to Christ for answers and guidance?

_____

_____

_____

FOR REFLECTION

Describe a time you encountered Jesus as Christ.

_____

_____

_____

Which characteristic of Christ draws you closer to God? Why?

_____

_____

_____

Which message from the devotions this week did you most need—and why?

_____

_____

_____

PERSONAL PRAYER

I praise You, Christ, for...

_____

_____

_____

Forgive me, Christ, when I...

_____

_____

_____

I'm grateful to You, Christ, for...

_____

_____

_____

Christ, today I need Your help to...

_____

_____

_____

When you see the word *Christ*—a name used more than five hundred times in the New Testament—you're reading the Old Testament word *Messiah*. The word *Messiah* literally means "the anointed one." It refers to the chosen one, called for a specific purpose and given the power to carry out that purpose from God Himself. The name Christ reflects the role of being chosen and empowered by God for His unique, anointed purpose.

Fully God, Fully Man

Truly this was the Son of God!

MATTHEW 27:54

How could Jesus be both fully God and fully human? Have you asked this question of a pastor or a mentor? If so, you aren't the first to do so, and you won't be the last.

The answer is found in the virgin birth. Mary's humanity came together with God's deity to create the most unique person in human history. And while Mary was human and her DNA contained the sinful human nature, it was the role of the Holy Spirit to not only merge in her to create human life but also to protect Jesus's human nature from receiving the sin nature (Luke 1:35). This resulted in Jesus's perfect duality, necessary for Him to carry out the unique prophetic plan of atonement God set in place following the fall of Adam.

It was prophesied that the woman's "seed" would crush the head of the devil (Genesis 3:15). This seems to have an inherent biological contradiction. After all, the seed of a man impregnates a woman. Never does the seed of a woman create new life.

Except in the case of Jesus.

The deity of heaven produced the Son of God and the Son of Man through the woman. Jesus possesses the natures of both God and man. He reveals to us the heart, goals, character, attributes, and desires of God. But He also identifies with our heart, goals, character, attributes, and desires as humans. This is why He could be hungry one moment and the next moment feed five thousand people. He could be thirsty one moment and the next moment walk on water. One moment He could die, then in another moment rise from the dead. And this is why we fall to our knees and say with our own mouths, "Truly this is the Son of God!"

———

Jesus, as both fully divine and fully human, You lead me to the Father, and You lead me to salvation. I am in awe that You chose to be both powerful and personal. Amen.

I'd Like to Be Closer to Abba

*Because you are sons, God has sent forth the Spirit of
His Son into our hearts, crying, "Abba! Father!"*

GALATIANS 4:6

Sin has messed up all of us. But Jesus's dual nature supplies you and me with the ability to withstand temptation and remove sin's grip on our lives. As the Son of God and the Son of Man, Jesus's relationship with God modeled a level of closeness that's open to each of us. While Jesus was on earth, He and God remained so familiar with each other that Jesus called God "Father."

It's interesting to note that when Jesus was on the cross, He referred to the Father as "God." When bearing all our sin, Jesus was separate from the intimacy He had known with the Father. God's holiness withdrew from Jesus. In Matthew 27:46, we read that the Son uttered these words: "My God, My God, why have You forsaken Me?" The one He knew as Daddy quickly became the great, looming deity we know as God.

This is what sin does in our lives: It severs intimacy. As Isaiah 59:2 puts it, "Your iniquities have made a separation between you and your God, and your sins have hidden His face from you so that He does not hear."

But the closer you get to Jesus, the closer you will get to God. In fact, as you draw nearer to Jesus, you'll soon come to know God on the level of "Daddy" too. Once you get to know the names Son of God and Son of Man and apply the reality of their truth in your life, you gain the ability to draw close to God in a way only the atonement of a sinless Savior could allow.

Through Jesus (Son of God and Son of Man), you can experience God as Father. You can call out to Abba Father with assurance, confidence, and the intimate love Jesus modeled for you.

———

Jesus, I have felt the separation caused by sin, and it's a dark, lonely experience. As Son of God and Son of Man, You are the way back to intimacy with the Father. Amen.

Your Dual Focus

Your kingdom come. Your will be done, on earth as it is in heaven.

MATTHEW 6:10

Most of us have too limited a view of Jesus's death. The majority believe that God became a man to take us to heaven—period.

But Jesus came, lived, died, and rose to do much more than that. Yes, He did come so you would have a way to heaven, but He also died and rose in order to bring heaven (its rule, authority, power, grace, confidence, compassion, wisdom, and more) to you on earth. Jesus came to render powerless the authority of the devil and to give you power over sin. When you accepted Jesus, the person and work of the Holy Spirit through Christ came into you.

But Jesus didn't secure your victory only for your sake. You are saved on earth from the authority of the devil so you can live out God's kingdom purpose for you. God has given you a divine destiny to fulfill. But far too many believers never live out their destinies because they fail to make the connection between salvation in time with God's purpose for that time.

Your life was never meant to be only about you.

You are to use your time, talents, and treasures to strategically advance God's kingdom on earth for His glory, your good, and others' benefit. Just as Jesus possessed a dual purpose as Son of God and Son of Man, once you become a follower of Jesus, you also have a dual focus. You are to set your thoughts on things above (Colossians 3:2)—preparing and planning for rewards in eternity—while also advancing the will of God on earth (today's verse). It's an important mission. But with the guidance and power of Jesus, you're equipped for the great things He has for you to do.

———

Jesus, when I look to You for guidance, You lead me to Your kingdom right here and now. What do You, as Son of God and Son of Man, call me to do today? Amen.

Greater Things

Jesus answered and said to him, "Because I said to you that
I saw you under the fig tree, do you believe? You will see
greater things than these." And He said to him, "Truly, truly, I
say to you, you will see the heavens opened and the angels
of God ascending and descending on the Son of Man."

JOHN 1:50-51

Once you recognize Jesus as the Son of God and come to believe in Him as a reflection of God Himself, you will gain access to the authority over all you need in your life on earth. The theology behind this statement is revealed in the story of Jesus, Philip, and Nathanael, found in the book of John. When Jesus asked Philip to follow Him, Philip realized Jesus was the one the prophets wrote about. So he told this to Nathanael, who was skeptical yet agreed to meet Jesus.

When Nathanael met Jesus, however, Jesus spoke to him as if He already knew him. This took Nathanael by surprise. Jesus explained He had seen him under the fig tree *before* Philip had even called him to come. Nathanael knew there was no way that could have happened apart from a supernatural work of God Himself. He believed immediately. He recognized the authority of Jesus as the Son of God and was told he would come to know the power and presence of the Son of Man. And because of Nathanael's belief, Jesus informed him he would get to see even greater things.

You might be waiting to experience the power of Jesus that you read about, sing about, and hear preached. You don't want Him to be real only far off in the heavenlies; you also want Him to be real right here in your realities. And God will be that for you—but only when you first honor and acknowledge Jesus as the Son of God, the exact reflection of God Himself.

When you remain in God's will, you see heaven's intervention in history. Jesus is both the Son of God and the Son of Man, connecting heaven with earth and providing you with all you need to live out your divine destiny.

Jesus, *I pray to walk in Your will because You are fully God. I am redeemed because, as Son of God and Son of Man, You connect me to eternity and to the Father. Amen.*

EXPERIENCE *the Son of God, Son of Man*

FOCUS SCRIPTURE

Since the children share in flesh and blood, He Himself likewise also partook of the same, that through death He might render powerless him who had the power of death, that is, the devil, and might free those who through fear of death were subject to slavery all their lives. For assuredly He does not give help to angels, but He gives help to the descendant of Abraham (Hebrews 2:14-16).

How have you experienced the help and the hope of the Son of God and Son of Man?

_____

_____

_____

FOR REFLECTION

Describe a time you encountered Jesus as the Son of God, Son of Man.

_____

_____

_____

Which characteristic of the Son of God, Son of Man draws you closer to God? Why?

_____

_____

_____

Which message from the devotions this week did you most need—and why?

_____

_____

_____

PERSONAL PRAYER

I praise You, Son of God, Son of Man, for…

_____

_____

_____

Forgive me, Son of God, Son of Man, when I…

_____

_____

_____

I'm grateful to You, Son of God, Son of Man, for…

_____

_____

_____

Son of God, Son of Man, today I need Your help to…

_____

_____

_____

Through Jesus, God has adopted us, so spiritually and legally He's our Father. God does not desire for Jesus to be an only child. He's a unique child, yes. He's a one-of-a-kind child, no doubt. But He's not the only child of God. As we draw near to Jesus and allow God's will to work in and through our lives, we become conformed to the image of Jesus and reflect Him as children of God (Romans 8:28-29).

From the Beginning

In the beginning was the Word,
and the Word was with God, and the Word was God.

JOHN 1:1

Have you ever wondered where everything came from? This isn't a lofty, silly question to ask. In fact, both the question and answer have a profound effect on us. Your belief about the origin of the world affects the way you think about your life, your choices, and your values.

Some believe there was basically *nothing* at the very beginning. But then following a "big bang," there was *something*. That *something* involved the particles that make up the building blocks of life. These, over the process of billions of years, evolved into everything we see today, including you and me.

While the theory of evolution keeps evolving as people hunt for scientific evidence to support it, at its core it suggests that God isn't necessary. That something came from nothing, and order came from chaos. Frankly, I think it takes a lot of faith to believe in the scenario that an impersonal process lies behind everything in our world.

Perhaps the appeal of the evolutionary theory for many people is that it dismisses our sense of accountability to a personal God who made us, is bigger than us, and can override our decisions. Evolution lets us believe we are our own god.

But the Bible tells a different story.

Our verse today reminds us that Jesus was there at the very first moment of creation. As the Word, Jesus is there on page one of history. Though He doesn't show up in His incarnate (human) form until well after the close of the Old Testament, He's been on the stage since before the curtains even opened. Don't miss the fullness of God's ongoing story by skipping the truth of how that story began and who was there. Something didn't come from nothing. You didn't come from nothing. Everything came from the God of everything.

———

Jesus, *it fills me with awe to know that You were there at the very beginning. As the Word, You were part of the world's creation just as You're here to create this life I live. Amen.*

Provider and Purpose of Life

The Word became flesh, and dwelt among us, and we saw His glory,
glory as of the only begotten of the Father, full of grace and truth.

JOHN 1:14

Friend, the Word has a history. He existed prior to the beginning. And the only thing that precedes the beginning is eternity. The Word was intimately face-to-face with God. In fact, it *was* God. So when we talk about the Word, we're talking about the self-revelation of God. The Word is not an impersonal force.

Whenever we see the name Word in Scripture, it references both the message of God and a person. God's Word is equal to God's person since the Word was God. The Word *is* God. John tells us that the Word became flesh. He was preexistent, coexistent, and self-existent, but He also became tangibly existent. Through Jesus, God introduced the physical manifestation of His rule and divinity into the creation He Himself had made.

The world was made by God through Jesus and for Jesus. Contrary to popular opinion, it was not made first and foremost for us. Jesus, the Word through whom God made creation, is the reason God made it in the first place:

> By [the Son] all things were created, both in the heavens and on earth, visible and invisible, whether thrones or dominions or rulers or authorities—all things have been created through Him and for Him. He is before all things, and in Him all things hold together (Colossians 1:16-17).

So when God created the world through Jesus, He gave it back to Him as a present. Understanding ownership of creation is critical to our finding peace, faith, and purpose. Jesus, the Word, represents the entire reason you exist. The secret to life is simply to give glory back to Jesus. Because when you do, He will infuse more life into you and whatever it is you're doing.

———

Jesus, *when I get lost in the small and big challenges of being human, I rest in Your presence as both God and God's message. You are the Word I abide in and am guided by. Amen.*

No Small Sacrifice

Although He existed in the form of God, [He] did not regard equality with God a thing to be grasped, but emptied Himself, taking the form of a bond-servant, and being made in the likeness of men.

PHILIPPIANS 2:6-7

Jesus walked the streets in Israel. He talked. He ate. He did all the things humans do, but He did them as the manifested Word—the revelation of God. According to Colossians 2:9, "In Him all the fullness of Deity dwells in bodily form." The fullness of God the Father resides in Jesus Christ.

Yet even though this fullness resides in Jesus, we learn something powerful about Him in today's passage. We discover that even though He was (and is) equal with God, He didn't allow His equality to keep Him from carrying out His responsibility. He recognized that He had a role to play, and He willingly carried out that role. When the passage says Jesus "emptied Himself," the phrase comes from the Greek word *kenóō*, which means "to pour out." He completely poured out His deity into humanity and became a slave to His purpose of bringing us salvation. He humbled Himself to the point of death so we could live.

This is why understanding this name of Jesus—the Word—is so critical. Because not just anyone emptied Himself out for service. No, this is the One through whom and by whom and for whom all things exist.

His is no small sacrifice. He didn't make it because He had nothing better to do. His is the greatest sacrifice of all time. And He gave it willingly so that He might accomplish the return of the King's rule over the hearts of mankind. He came to bring life where life was not found. He did it for people back then, and He still does it for us today. The source of life itself gave up His life so that you and I can live.

———

Jesus, it's hard to imagine willingly letting go of the ultimate power in order to save others. I am humbled by Your love and grateful for the gift of eternal life. Amen.

Your Power Source

In the beginning God created the heavens and the earth. The earth was formless and void, and darkness was over the surface of the deep, and the Spirit of God was moving over the surface of the waters. Then God said, "Let there be light"; and there was light.

GENESIS 1:1-3

As you come to know Jesus according to the name Word, you come face-to-face with His creative and life-giving power. We don't often associate these attributes with Jesus. Somehow we have this notion that God created and ran everything for Himself, and then Jesus showed up centuries later. But this name places Jesus not only as an active participant in the creation process but also as the very reason creation was made. He is the giver and receiver of life.

To apply this attribute of Jesus to your own life, you must first understand that this name animates life. By tapping into the Word, you tap into the source and purpose of life. One of the reasons more Christians don't see the movement of God in their lives is that they won't allow Jesus to carry out what He accomplished. Jesus is the light of life, but His thoughts, perspective, heart, and intentions must be made to bear on your thoughts, perspective, heart, and intentions.

The Word is God incarnate. The Word is life. The Word is light. Like oxygen to the lungs and cells in the body, the Word has all we need to live our life abundantly. Only in the intentional, ongoing pursuit of His presence, purpose, power, and perspective through abiding in His written Word (the Bible) and with His Spirit will you experience the fullness of life you desire.

Pursue intimacy with Jesus through His Word, and you'll get life as part of the package (John 17:3). Because from the beginning, Jesus has been the life, light, and living manifestation of deity who sits over all, orders all, and holds all of life together. As you go about your day, think of Jesus not only as your power source but as the one who holds your life together.

———

Jesus, impress upon me Your thoughts, perspective, heart, and intentions. These aren't merely words; these are characteristics and powers of the Word I have access to. Amen.

EXPERIENCE *the Word*

FOCUS SCRIPTURE

God, after He spoke long ago to the fathers in the prophets in many portions and in many ways, in these last days has spoken to us in His Son, whom He appointed heir of all things, through whom also He made the world (Hebrews 1:1-2).

God made the world through Jesus, the Word. What is God creating in you through the Word?

_____

_____

_____

FOR REFLECTION

Describe a time you encountered Jesus as the Word.

_____

_____

_____

Which characteristic of the Word draws you closer to God? Why?

_____

_____

_____

Which message from the devotions this week did you most need—and why?

_____

_____

_____

PERSONAL PRAYER

I praise You, Jesus, as the Word, for…

_____

_____

_____

Forgive me, Jesus, as the Word, when I…

_____

_____

_____

I'm grateful to You, Jesus, as the Word, for…

_____

_____

_____

Jesus, as the Word, today I need Your help to…

_____

_____

_____

The Greek translation of *word* is *logos*. *Logos* was a powerful word in Jesus's day, because the Greeks used that word to define the impersonal force behind the universe. When they spoke about the *logos*, it was in the context of identifying a creative force that gave rise to all knowledge, wisdom, and even creation.

HOLY SPIRIT

I have many more things to say to you, but you cannot bear them now. But when He, the Spirit of truth, comes, He will guide you into all the truth; for He will not speak on His own initiative, but whatever He hears, He will speak; and He will disclose to you what is to come. He will glorify Me, for He will take of Mine and will disclose it to you. All things that the Father has are Mine; therefore I said that He takes of Mine and will disclose it to you.

JOHN 16:12-15

Spirit of Truth

The Spirit has a central role in the life of the believer and the empowerment of the church, with the distinctive task of making the reality and truth of God experienced in both. And because He possesses emotions, intellect, and will, He is to be related to on a personal level. He's to be *known*, not merely considered a force or power to be manipulated or used. Although He's nonmaterial, intangible, and invisible, He is nonetheless real and relational.

As with the other two members of the Trinity, one of the best means to understand, appreciate, and benefit from the person of the Holy Spirit is to explore the names and attribute descriptions He's given in Scripture. They explain how He lives those roles in us, through us, and for us.

When we come to know the Spirit, we can more intimately understand the unique ways God reveals Himself to us. To what degree we take the person and work of the Holy Spirit seriously is the degree to which we will experience more of God.

While some of the Holy Spirit's names and descriptions are not always capitalized as proper nouns as I write—just as they aren't in Scripture—they are nevertheless as significant to our journey of discovery.

As you spend time with these selected names, my prayer is that you will relate to the person of the Holy Spirit in a more personal and intimate way. And that you will learn how to take full advantage of all the Spirit offers. Friend, when you grasp how to do this, His availability and presence and power will be maximized in your physical life, emotional life, and most importantly, your spiritual life.

You Know Him

I will ask the Father, and He will give you another Helper,
that He may be with you forever.

JOHN 14:16

Have you ever been in a spiritual slump? Maybe you're in one today. Jesus knew there would be days, weeks, or even years when His people would feel disconnected and at a loss as to how to live. He especially knew this would happen to His own band of close disciples when He was crucified and then left their physical presence. That's why He called them aside to meet with them in a secluded room, where He talked about what He planned to do about it. He wanted to give them the tools to thrive even when He was no longer physically by their side. Stories like this remind us today how God is always providing what we need.

Jesus also knew His disciples were sad and scared. He assured them, "Do not let your heart be troubled" (John 14:1) and told them He was going ahead to prepare a place for them. Then He introduced the person and work of the Holy Spirit through the interesting phrase *another Helper*. This was to emphasize the reality that even though He was leaving them, God was sending someone exactly like Him to help them through each upcoming day, week, month, and year. In being similar, He, the Holy Spirit, would also bear all the attributes of deity Christ had.

Jesus sees our fears, our sorrows, and our spiritual slumps. He worries about us feeling alone in our journeys. That's why He sent the Helper, and we know Him. We don't get to walk with Jesus in the flesh, but we do get to walk with Him every day of our lives when we faithfully walk with the Holy Spirit. Trust the Helper and the comfort and guidance He offers to you no matter what you face.

———

Holy Spirit, when God sent You so many years ago, He provided the comfort and guidance I would need today. Your help is with me no matter where I go. Amen.

Never Alone

You know Him because He abides with you and will be in you.

JOHN 14:17

Do you believe that your help is right here, right now? The Holy Spirit is close enough to be with you in an experiential way. He is by your side, like a partner or a companion. Not only that, but He's also in you. This means the Holy Spirit walks *alongside* you while at the same time He makes His home *inside* you. And while you may feel alone at times, this reality of the Holy Spirit's closeness to you both near and within means you're never truly alone.

From the moment you trusted in Jesus Christ for salvation from your sins, you received the companionship of the Holy Spirit both externally and internally. The reason He remains present in both locations is that, depending on the situation, you can need help in both areas of your life at the same time. Whether you're facing something in your external circumstances or struggling with internal thoughts or emotions, the Holy Spirit has positioned Himself to be available to you when and where you need Him the most.

When Jesus revealed the plan for the Holy Spirit to join the disciples, He lovingly said, "I will not leave you as orphans; I will come to you" (John 14:18). Perhaps you know what it is to be an orphan. Or you know what it is to have parents or others who are absent emotionally. Jesus makes it clear that He will not abandon us or distance Himself from us.

Satan would like for you to forget that. He would like you to feel isolated and without help. And when you feel that way, it's easy to give up and lose hope. But when you remember the closeness of the helper God has given you, you'll know you can get through anything life sends your way—without a doubt. You are not alone.

———

Holy Spirit, though it's easy to feel isolated and abandoned in this chaotic and cold world, with You I need not be afraid. I'm eternally grateful for Your presence. Amen.

Your Comforter and Advocate

The Helper, the Holy Spirit, whom the Father will send
in My name, He will teach you all things, and bring
to your remembrance all that I said to you.

JOHN 14:26

The Holy Spirit knows what you need and when you need it, especially when you need it and Him the most. Just two months after my wife of nearly 50 years passed, I was scheduled to film a Bible study in Sedona, Arizona. In the years prior to her becoming ill, Lois and I had enjoyed traveling to various places around the world to film these studies.

But this journey would be different. After the plane landed, I walked alone. I pulled my luggage alone. My head hung down, and my heart joined it. With each step, I grew more discouraged. I didn't want to do this without Lois. Nor did I feel like teaching on the Bible at that moment.

But the Holy Spirit met me right where I was with just what I needed to keep going. A lovely couple prayed over me. Hotel staff greeted me with condolences while also offering words of spiritual encouragement. At every turn, I was lifted and held by the Holy Spirit in His roles of Comforter and Advocate.

I was able to do the teaching as planned. And while it was one of the more difficult things I've ever had to do, I found the subject of knowing God encouraging as I taught through it. In this space of great loss, as I remained obedient to Him despite the pain I was feeling, God peeled back the layers of pain and grief enough to help me see His presence in His Spirit like I needed to.

This didn't happen because I'm a pastor. Friend, this happened because I'm a child of God who has received the Helper—just like you. Look for Him in your grief and heartache. He's there for you too.

———

Holy Spirit, I'm grateful that You seek ways to bring me comfort and relief. When my spirit is discouraged and the burdens are great, You make Your presence known. Amen.

Hanging Out with the Holy Spirit

I tell you the truth, it is to your advantage that I go away; for if I do not go away, the Helper will not come to you; but if I go, I will send Him to you.

JOHN 16:7

The Holy Spirit, as the third person of the Trinity, is not an "it." He's not just a "power" to turn on and use. He's a person present both alongside each of us and within us. And as a person, He desires for you to relate to Him as much as anyone else would want you to relate to them.

If you desire this, too, it will involve your intentionally abiding with Him. To abide with the Spirit means you're hanging with Him. It means He's involved in the totality of your life. You're connecting with Him all the time. We're to bring the Spirit of God to bear in all we do. Whether we're driving, working, shopping, or spending time with family or in entertainment, we're to be conversing with the Holy Spirit (praying) at all times.

As hard as it was for Jesus to leave the disciples, He knew it was to their advantage to have the Helper in His place. Jesus faced the physical limits of His full humanity. But because the Holy Spirit is nonmaterial, He can be everywhere at all times. He can be advocating for you the same time He's advocating for me. He can guide us. He brings things to our minds and helps us remember them. He teaches us. He convicts us. He strengthens us. He also searches the deep things of God and brings them to our awareness. And when He does, He can make connections we never even knew to make or open doors we didn't even have the ability to knock on.

Go toward God by walking with the Spirit and talking with the Spirit. Hang out with the Helper 24/7. When you do that, you'll unleash the Holy Spirit's power in you in ways you never even imagined.

Holy Spirit, because You're not restricted by the limits of the physical world, Your help is limitless. Today I celebrate the ways You lead, inspire, and teach me. Amen.

EXPERIENCE *the Helper*

FOCUS SCRIPTURE

When the Helper comes, whom I will send to you from the Father, that is the Spirit of truth who proceeds from the Father, He will testify about Me (John 15:26).

How has the Helper taught you personally about Jesus and the Father?

_____

_____

_____

FOR REFLECTION

Describe a time you encountered the Holy Spirit as the Helper.

_____

_____

_____

Which characteristic of the Helper draws you closer to God? Why?

_____

_____

_____

Which message from the devotions this week did you most need—and why?

_____

_____

_____

PERSONAL PRAYER

I praise You, Spirit, as the Helper, for…

_____

_____

_____

Forgive me, Spirit, as the Helper, when I…

_____

_____

_____

I'm grateful to You, Spirit, as the Helper, for…

_____

_____

_____

Spirit, as the Helper, today I need Your help to…

_____

_____

_____

Over and over again, we read that the Holy Spirit's role is that of a helper. The original word in Greek is *parakletos*. *Parakletos* is ripe with meaning, referencing one who is uniquely gifted to come alongside another and assist. When the Holy Spirit shows up as the Helper, Advocate, or Comforter, He comes with the ability to intervene when situations or circumstances have been stirred up by Satan, aimed at hurting or destroying you.

A New Day of Blessing

The Holy Spirit descended upon Him in bodily form
like a dove, and a voice came out of heaven, "You are
My beloved Son, in You I am well-pleased."

LUKE 3:22

In today's verse, Luke tells us the Spirit appeared "in bodily form"—as a dove, revealing that the Spirit can take on the form of substance on earth, as a dove or a human being or anything else He desires to present Himself.

I had a hint of this early in my grief process after losing Lois to cancer. On a particularly hard day, a friend brought lunch to my house, sat with me, and prayed for me. He said God had put me on his mind and heart in such a way that he knew he needed to reach out.

While my friend was and still is definitely a human being, I believe through him the Holy Spirit showed up for me in my grief. God knows what we need and when we need it while simultaneously meeting that need through the ministry of the Holy Spirit as a helper, yes, but also, at times, as "a dove."

God chose a dove for Noah to send out to see if the waters had subsided after the flood (Genesis 8:9-12). The second time the dove came back, an olive leaf in its mouth provided evidence that the waters had subsided enough for vegetation to form. The dove brought with it a testimony of renewal for everyone there to see.

This is why we often see the image of a dove with an olive branch tied to events involving peace agreements or restoration. The dove symbolizes the end of judgment and the onset of a new day of blessing and freedom, reminding us that something new lies ahead when we're emerging from struggle. Trust me, friend, the Holy Spirit does this for us too. Watch for His comfort to come to you when you need it most.

———

Holy Spirit, You have brought me comfort through the words and actions of others. I lean into Your presence today, grateful for the restoration You bring. Amen.

Peace-Seeking, Peace-Giving

Do not grieve the Holy Spirit of God, by whom you were sealed
for the day of redemption. Let all bitterness and wrath and
anger and clamor and slander be put away from you, along with
all malice. Be kind to one another, tender-hearted, forgiving
each other, just as God in Christ also has forgiven you.

EPHESIANS 4:30-32

Because doves are one of the most sensitive birds in God's creation, if they come to bird feeders or trees in your yard, they're among the first birds to fly off when you walk outside. God, of course, knew about this sensitivity when He chose to descend to earth as the Holy Spirit in the bodily form of a dove.

For the dove to have felt free enough to rest on Jesus at His baptism, then, says a lot. A dove won't get anywhere close to conflict, whether it senses it or witnesses it. A dove will land only where it senses great peace and safety. A dove hangs out in places that are serene. A dove doesn't linger or loiter in an agitated atmosphere. That's why it's significant that a dove descended on Jesus to symbolize the affirmation from the Father, resting on Him as the Father saying He was well-pleased with His Son.

Just like the dove in nature, the Dove that is the Holy Spirit is sensitive. He is peace, calm, and stability. And because the Dove is sealed in you as a child of God, His misery will show up as your misery. His unhappiness will show up as your unhappiness. If you want to experience the peace, comfort, and calm the Spirit has to give you, you need to be aware enough not to offend or grieve Him.

Be aware of what you say and how you say it. Be aware of what you think and how it affects your behavior. Be aware of your choices with regard to what you see, read, watch, scroll through, or discuss. Be mindful of what grieves the Spirit, and then seek to reduce or remove those things in your life. That's when you'll begin to experience His presence bringing you the peace you long for.

Holy Spirit, may I nurture a kind and pure spirit so I do not grieve You. Let me not offend You with actions that are hateful, hurtful, or harmful. I long for Your calm. Amen.

Don't Give Satan an Opportunity

Laying aside falsehood, speak truth each one of you
with his neighbor, for we are members of one another.
Be angry, and yet do not sin; do not let the sun go down
on your anger, and do not give the devil an opportunity.

EPHESIANS 4:25-27

When the Holy Spirit is unhappy within you, how are you to be happy? One of the reasons Satan seeks to keep us in a state of chaos is so the Holy Spirit won't function in His full capacity. Many of us live in a perpetual cycle of discomfort because we've alienated the Holy Spirit through our choices. Rather than address the trigger of grief within them, people try to escape the unhappiness with distractions such as entertainment, food, sex, drugs, spending, religion, exercise—you name it.

The Holy Spirit is as sensitive as a dove and reacts quickly to what isn't consistent with His nature. But because He's been "sealed" in us, He can't fly off. Rather, He remains in a grieving state inside us, and this rises up within our own souls and spirits, manifesting in emotional, circumstantial, and spiritual chaos.

Friend, don't open the door for the devil by using poor judgment when it comes to your speech, actions, thoughts, and intentions. When you steal from someone, you're stealing from the Spirit. When you defraud someone, you're defrauding the Spirit. When you dismiss someone, you're dismissing the Spirit. Each of us is made in the image of God. To harm or marginalize anyone is to do the same to God.

We read that as God continued His creation of the world, "the Spirit of God was hovering over the waters" (Genesis 1:2 NIV). Like a dove soaring, the Spirit hovered in order to bring order out of the chaos. We should want a close connection with the Spirit because He can bring order out of chaos. When you align your heart with the Dove, He will bring order out of your mess, your grief, your pain. He will usher in order and calm where you thought there would forever be pain.

———

Holy Spirit, help me release the distractions I use to avoid the cause of my discomfort and the source of Your grief. May my life align with Your gentle nature. Amen.

Keep the Fire Going

Rejoice always, pray continually, give thanks in all circumstances;
for this is God's will for you in Christ Jesus. Do not quench
the Spirit. Do not treat prophecies with contempt but test
them all; hold on to what is good, reject every kind of evil.

1 THESSALONIANS 5:16-22 NIV

The Holy Spirit is positioned to bring you great hope, calm, power, and peace but only when you choose not to quench Him with how you live your life.

Quenching the Spirit is similar to pouring water on a fire. The fire can no longer produce the warmth or benefit it was once intended to give. Far too often we choose to quench the Spirit rather than respond to Him. When He's been grieved and creates discomfort within our souls, we decide we don't want Him bothering us. We don't want Him convicting or guiding us. So we put the fire out.

In other words, we reject the teaching. We reject the leading. We reject the restraint. We decide that telling others exactly how we feel in order to let it all out is more important than listening to and responding to the Spirit. In essence, we tell the Dove to shut up because we're passionate about whatever issue we're facing.

One of the most common reasons Christians don't experience answered prayer as much as they possibly can is they're living a lifestyle of conflict in relationships, in opposition to God's truth, or in what they say and how they say it. Conflict closes the door on prayer because the Spirit, like a dove, doesn't operate in an environment of chaos.

God has placed the Holy Spirit in every believer. It's up to you to choose to pursue intimacy with the Dove on an ongoing basis. He is sealed within you, available as you intentionally cultivate closeness through aligning with the truth and love of God. Friend, choose to keep that fire burning with a heart of gratitude and humility.

———

Holy Spirit, are You at peace within me? With thanksgiving, I will open the door to Your truth and conviction by surrendering my will and seeking Your own. Amen.

EXPERIENCE *the Dove*

FOCUS SCRIPTURE

James explained the connection between conflict and our relational intimacy with God, especially the Holy Spirit, when He wrote,

> Do you not know that friendship with the world is hostility toward God? Therefore whoever wishes to be a friend of the world makes himself an enemy of God. Or do you think that the Scripture speaks to no purpose: "He jealously desires the Spirit which He has made to dwell in us"? (James 4:4-5).

What's one way you can let go of your friendship with the world to have greater connection with the Dove?

_____

_____

FOR REFLECTION

Describe a time you encountered the Holy Spirit as the Dove.

_____

_____

Which characteristic of the Dove draws you closer to God? Why?

_____

_____

Which message from the devotions this week did you most need—and why?

_____

_____

_____

PERSONAL PRAYER

I praise You, Spirit, as the Dove, for…

_____

_____

_____

Forgive me, Spirit, as the Dove, when I…

_____

_____

_____

I'm grateful to You, Spirit, as the Dove, for…

_____

_____

_____

Spirit, as the Dove, today I need Your help to…

_____

_____

_____

The biblical image of a dove provides rest and calm. As David wrote in Psalm 55:6, "Oh, that I had wings like a dove! I would fly away and be at rest." This picture of the dove going away to a restful place stirs hope in our hearts and reminds us that one of the reasons God often feels far away is that we operate in or create an environment where His Holy Spirit isn't comfortable. This happens in our homes, marriages, friendships, churches, and work environments—and especially in our thoughts.

Are You Thirsty?

On the last day, the great day of the feast, Jesus stood and cried
out, saying, "If anyone is thirsty, let him come to Me and drink."

JOHN 7:37

What physical water is to the body, spiritual water is to the soul. If you starve the body of physical water, it won't work right. If you starve the soul of spiritual water, it won't work right.

Jesus introduces us to this concept of spiritual water in the context of the Feast of Tabernacles. God had instructed the Jewish people to take part in this great feast in order to remind themselves of their journey through the wilderness.

One of the more traumatic occurrences during that trip was their running out of water. Another occurrence was when they thought they were trapped at the edge of the Red Sea. Yet in both situations God had shown up for them in miraculous ways. At the Red Sea, He parted the water for them to cross to safety. In the wilderness, He let water gush out of a rock so they could quench their thirst.

For the Feast of Tabernacles, the Israelites had been instructed to build booths, similar to what we call tents. They erected a tented city to live in during this feast, time established and set aside from the normal routines for the people to reflect on how God had supplied them through their season of need.

Obviously, some of the provisions God supplied during these years had to do with water. Thus, when Jesus unveils this next truth symbol and character quality—Living Water—He's using language relevant to their understanding of dependence on God.

Are you thirsty for the Holy Spirit? For God's provision and life? Jesus tells the Israelites and you and me that the Living Water is available to us during and after our personal wilderness season. We can always draw what we need and know it will fill and fuel us for the journey forward.

———

Holy Spirit, I am so weary, and my spirit is dry. I come to You, the Living Water, ready to be satisfied and refreshed. In my season of need, You quench my thirsty spirit. Amen.

The Source Within

"He who believes in Me, as the Scripture said, 'From his innermost being will flow rivers of living water.'" But this He spoke of the Spirit, whom those who believed in Him were to receive; for the Spirit was not yet given, because Jesus was not yet glorified.

JOHN 7:38-39

It's easy to tell when our bodies are thirsty. Parched lips and a sluggish feeling alert us to our need to drink. It's equally easy to tell when the soul is depleted. Your spiritual thirst makes itself known through dissatisfaction, discontentment, unforgiveness, rampant sin, confusion, internal chaos, and more.

Because the need for spiritual water is so profound, it causes us to always be on the lookout for how to meet that need. And Satan likes to send us on chases or in circles aimed at locating cheap and bogus substitutes that were never designed to exist as authentic thirst quenchers. In fact, Satan doesn't mind if you confuse religion and spiritual ritual with the living water, because they will never meet your need either.

We often wind up drinking spiritual saltwater instead of the pure water Jesus came to give and the Holy Spirit supplies. This undrinkable substitute for the real thing comes in the forms of illegitimate relationships, illegitimate entertainment, illegitimate ego boosts, and more illegitimate "solutions." At first, these versions might seem to satisfy, but sooner or later we realize we're thirstier than when we started.

Only the Spirit offers you and me the living water of Christ, which we need for our souls to not only survive but thrive. But so many of us are waiting on the Holy Spirit to come and pour the living water down our dry throats instead of making our way to reach the source Jesus provides. When you experience a craving of discontent welling up within you or notice spiritual issues unresolved, you need to seek and drink the living water available to you in your innermost being. This is our certain, safe, and sustainable source of spiritual water. Come and drink and be refreshed!

Holy Spirit, for too long I've sought refreshment from the shallow, polluted waters of the world. You are the only source for spiritual hydration, and I give You glory. Amen.

You Need to Take a Drink

He said to me, "It is done. I am the Alpha and the Omega,
the beginning and the end. I will give to the one who thirsts
from the spring of the water of life without cost."

REVELATION 21:6

Coming to Jesus is what you and I did when we came to Him for salvation. But the action we often forget once saved is that we still need to "drink."

When I preached on this subject at the church where I pastor in Dallas, I held a cup full of water as I talked about this passage. The water was pure. It had cost me nothing. But just holding the water and talking about it would do nothing for me. Not until I drank the water would my body be refreshed and my physical needs be met.

It's a simple but profound illustration. You and I can have spiritual water freely given to us and still remain unsatisfied. To drink of the spiritual water Jesus came to supply through the Spirit means you and I must appropriate this living water into the internal operation of our lives.

If you've accepted Jesus Christ for salvation so you're bound for heaven when you die, that's great. But you must not allow that eternal security to lull you into complacency while on earth. Eternal salvation isn't sufficient for healing and satiating a thirsty soul during your journey as a human being. To do that, you must come to Jesus and appropriate the living water He offers into your daily existence. And when you do, this living water becomes more than just something you have access to; it's something you're using and benefiting from.

Jesus gives to us from the water of life at no cost because the cost has already been paid. It's been placed inside of you through the work Jesus Christ did on the cross. The deliverance you desire is already within you. The guidance you desire is already within you. The grace you desire is already within you. You just need to drink.

———

Holy Spirit, I won't go on and on about my dry spiritual season when I have yet to drink from the eternal spring Jesus made possible. Time to stop talking and start sipping. Amen.

Keep It Flowing

The Spirit and the bride say, "Come." And let the one who hears say, "Come." And let the one who is thirsty come; let the one who wishes take the water of life without cost.

REVELATION 22:17

You can know a person has tapped into the living water when you see the free flow of kindness, patience, peace, encouraging words, and service.

And the opposite is true as well. You can tell when a person isn't connected to the Holy Spirit when they struggle to be nice. They serve themselves. They use harmful language. They no longer share any good with others because they no longer have any good within. They're spiritually dehydrated.

When I was a young boy growing up in Baltimore, we knew we could always go swimming on Saturdays—at least a form of swimming. During the summer weekends, the fire marshal opened up the local fire hydrant, water gushed out, and we had a temporary water park in the hood.

I asked my dad how a small fire hydrant could have all that water coming out of it. He told me the hydrant didn't hold the water; it was just a mechanism through which the water from a reservoir flowed. So when the fire marshal came around, all he did was open up the tap, making it possible for an abundance of water to come pouring through.

When we're connected to the reservoir of the Holy Spirit, the water will not only flow but continue to gush out as long as we keep the tap open. And we do that by glorifying Jesus Christ both privately and publicly. We keep it open by abiding in His presence. We keep the water running by aligning our hearts with God and allowing the Spirit's presence to produce His character within us. When that happens, other people will benefit as well from the life-giving water that not only flows in us but through us. Come. Take the water of life. And let it gush forth.

———

Holy Spirit, I will come to You daily to draw from Your reservoir. Living Water, as Your goodness and love flow in and through me to others, I give You praise. Amen.

EXPERIENCE *the Living Water*

FOCUS SCRIPTURE

I will pour out water on the thirsty land and streams on the dry ground; I will pour out My Spirit on your offspring and My blessing on your descendants (Isaiah 44:3).

How has the Living Water refreshed you recently?

_____

_____

_____

FOR REFLECTION

Describe a time you encountered the Holy Spirit as the Living Water.

_____

_____

_____

Which characteristic of the Living Water draws you closer to God? Why?

_____

_____

_____

Which message from the devotions this week did you most need—and why?

_____

_____

_____

PERSONAL PRAYER

I praise You, Spirit, as the Living Water, for…

_____

_____

_____

Forgive me, Spirit, as the Living Water, when I…

_____

_____

_____

I'm grateful to You, Spirit, as the Living Water, for…

_____

_____

_____

Spirit, as the Living Water, today I need Your help to…

_____

_____

_____

When you receive Christ, God places a pump inside your human spirit otherwise known as the Holy Spirit. Through Jesus, the Holy Spirit invades your human spirit and gives you spiritual life. The Spirit resides in the soul. The soul resides in the body. As the Holy Spirit pumps living water into your spirit, which then overflows into your soul, it offers you healing, contentment, order, strength, and purpose.

More Than a Feeling

You know of Jesus of Nazareth, how God anointed Him with the
Holy Spirit and with power, and how He went about doing good and
healing all who were oppressed by the devil, for God was with Him.

ACTS 10:38

If you've been in church for any length of time, you've heard the words *the anointing* or the phrase *the anointed one*. Over these next few days, we'll be present to the Holy Spirit as "the Anointing." This term speaks to a specific work of the Holy Spirit you certainly don't want to leave home without. It's a key feature of the Spirit's work in our lives.

For many people, the concept of the anointing boils down to an emotional experience—when they feel something tied to a spiritual thought or situation in church, in prayer, when in Scripture, or anytime, really. Oftentimes when people talk to me after church, I'll hear comments like, "That was an anointed sermon, Pastor," or "You really had the anointing today, Pastor."

More often than not, what those individuals are referencing is that they experienced an emotional reaction or an emotional impact based on what they heard.

While the Spirit does create anointed moments in ministry, I caution you to not relate every emotional reaction to a belief in the anointing. Many people—whether preachers, singers, or podcasters—elicit an emotional response simply with their own talents. Or your particular emotional response could be tied to something you're going through at that moment. While the Spirit does show up in these experiences, I also think people often limit the anointing to emotional reactions rather than coming to understand that the anointing goes much deeper. As we'll discover, it involves more than emotion. It involves the deep work of the Spirit in your life. It's the inner-working of the Spirit that enables and empowers the outer-working of tangible good works. You won't want to miss the power of the anointing.

———

Holy Spirit, Your power is so much more than an emotional high or special moment. I humbly ask You to empower me for good works that glorify God. Amen.

You've Got It

You have an anointing from the Holy One, and you all know. I
have not written to you because you do not know the truth, but
because you do know it, and because no lie is of the truth.

1 JOHN 2:20-21

What you need to remember about the anointing is that you already have it. If you're saved and trust in Jesus Christ for the forgiveness of your sins, you possess the anointing within you. You don't have to go looking for it. And you don't have to cross off a certain number of items on a checklist in order to gain it, because it's a gift.

In the Old Testament dispensation, the Holy Spirit would come and go. He would visit a person or situation, do His work, and then leave. But in the New Testament and ultimately in the church age, Jesus gave us the Holy Spirit as a permanent resident in our lives. He is within. And He is constant. First Corinthians 6:19 states it like this: "Do you not know that your body is a temple of the Holy Spirit who is in you, whom you have from God, and that you are not your own?"

Unfortunately, many Christians don't know they have the anointing. Thus, they don't know how to use it, and as a result, they fail to maximize any benefits. We all have a perfect resident within our human spirit, but we must learn to allow the Spirit to guide, direct, and infuse our lives with His anointing.

When the Holy Spirit is free to invade our human spirits, our souls get healed. Thus, if you want to fix your body, you first must clean up your soul. And if you want to clean up your soul, you have to open the pathway for the Holy Spirit to speak to your spirit by intentionally pursuing and accessing the anointing within. Only when the anointing enters and expands within you will your human spirit become perfected and pure.

Holy Spirit, please guide, direct, and infuse my life with Your power. I'm sorry for the times I've blocked the pathway to anointing. Today, I listen with an open heart. Amen.

Lighting Up God's Truth

To us God revealed them through the Spirit;
for the Spirit searches all things, even the depths of God.

1 CORINTHIANS 2:10

Do you have dimmer switches in your home? They bring the light in a room up or down. Well, God has given every believer a dimmer switch called the anointing. It's the role of the Holy Spirit to progressively bring the light of God's truth into your life.

Now, you may choose to keep this switch turned low with the light of God's truth coming to you dimly. But if you want to experience the full expression of God's truth—and His love—turn that switch up to its maximum level. This will enable you to see from God's perspective: "Things which eye has not seen and ear has not heard, and which have not entered the heart of man, all that God has prepared for those who love Him" (1 Corinthians 2:9).

This passage isn't talking about heaven. It reminds us of all we have access to while on earth. Yet we know only what God has prepared for those who love Him when we intentionally pursue and access the Spirit's anointing. When the anointing is turned on and the dimmer switch is turned up, you're free to see things normal human eyes can't see. You get to hear things normal human ears can't hear. You get to think things normal human minds can't even fathom.

In other words, the anointing pulls you from the physical realm into the spiritual realm so you can perceive, experience, see, and sense that which is from God Himself. The Spirit dips into the mind of God and brings to the mind of humanity these spiritual thoughts and spiritual words, which is the truth of Scripture.

Don't live limited by your five senses. Turn up that switch to discern and embrace the light of all God wants you to know, understand, and believe.

Holy Spirit, let me turn up that dimmer switch in my life. I don't want to live in the dark when I have access to Your truth, Lord. Flood my heart and life with Your light. Amen.

Spiritual Sight

As for you, the anointing which you received from Him abides
in you, and you have no need for anyone to teach you; but as
His anointing teaches you about all things, and is true and is
not a lie, and just as it has taught you, you abide in Him.

1 JOHN 2:27

When issues arise and our first question isn't *What does God say about this matter?*, then we are not abiding. You and I must do more than visit the Spirit. We must do more than attend church on Sundays. God does not desire weekend visitation from us. We must abide in His presence, pray without ceasing, and seek to align our hearts and minds with His viewpoint on every subject based on His Word.

As abiding and accessing the anointing becomes your lifestyle and you agree with God's revelation, the Holy Spirit will give you divine illumination so you can experience personal transformation. You'll be able to see things as you ought to see them, through spiritual eyes. As the psalmist writes, "Open my eyes, that I may behold wonderful things from Your law" (Psalm 119:18). You will come to understand God's Word for yourself when you fully access the anointing within you.

When you can see what's going on in the spiritual realm, your fears will dissipate. Your anxiety will fade. Your need for control will release itself in surrender to God. When you live spiritually, you get to see things spiritually.

God is always in the midst of what's going on. We just can't always see Him, because we've become so used to using our physical senses rather than tapping into the Spirit's anointing in us. You have access to Him right now. You have access to spiritual sight right now. That access has been given to you through the anointing within. But it's up to you whether you choose to use it. Then you must act on the truth of God as revealed in Scripture. The Holy Spirit will then clarify and empower your understanding and experience of God's truth in your life.

———

Holy Spirit, I've been missing out on accessing Your wisdom and clarity by not abiding in You daily. I want to see and understand with spiritual eyes. Amen.

EXPERIENCE *the Anointing*

FOCUS SCRIPTURE

We have received, not the spirit of the world, but the Spirit who is from God, so that we may know the things freely given to us by God, which things we also speak, not in words taught by human wisdom, but in those taught by the Spirit, combining spiritual thoughts with spiritual words (1 Corinthians 2:12-13).

What spiritual thoughts and truths have emerged in your life as you've experienced the Anointing?

_____

_____

_____

FOR REFLECTION

Describe a time you encountered the Holy Spirit as the Anointing.

_____

_____

_____

Which characteristic of the Anointing draws you closer to God? Why?

_____

_____

_____

Which message from the devotions this week did you most need—and why?

_____

_____

_____

PERSONAL PRAYER

I praise You, Spirit, as the Anointing, for...

_____

_____

_____

Forgive me, Spirit, as the Anointing, when I...

_____

_____

_____

I'm grateful to You, Spirit, as the Anointing, for...

_____

_____

_____

Spirit, as the Anointing, today I need Your help to...

_____

_____

_____

God, the Father, was the point person in Old Testament times. Jesus, the Son, became the point person on earth during the period of the Gospels. And the Holy Spirit is the point person now, during this time we call the church age. He's the third member of the Trinity, assigned to act on our behalf while we're on earth and to help us do the work God desires to be done here.

Don't Block the Spirit

Do not get drunk with wine, for that is
dissipation, but be filled with the Spirit.

EPHESIANS 5:18

If you're going to gain access to the will of God so you can leverage your life to confront evil and bring about good, you must be filled with the Spirit.

In Ephesians, Paul states this as a passive command. Meaning, it refers to something you *allow* to be done, not something you do yourself. So when Paul urges you and me to be filled, he's actually urging us to not block the Holy Spirit from filling us. He's urging us to allow the Spirit to do what only the Spirit can do in us. We must stop resisting the work of the Holy Spirit, because in releasing Him to work within us, we discover the power He has to supply.

Just like you would expect every car to have fuel, God expects every Christian to be full of the Spirit. A car without fuel is a useless car. Likewise, a Christian without the filling of the Spirit is a useless Christian. And just like a car, the moment we leave the source of our spiritual fuel, that fuel starts to burn away. Unfortunately, far too many people rely on the filling to take place at a church service. But if that isn't happening 24/7, you won't be in much of a good spot when it comes to living out your life. That kind of filling, the kind that's reliant on those around you to serve as a catalyst, doesn't last.

God's Spirit within you enables you to maximize your life for Him. The Holy Spirit provides what you need even in ways you didn't know you needed it. Friend, each day, decide to not block the Spirit so you can stay full and fueled for all the good work God has for you to do.

———

Holy Spirit, why do I hold back from embracing the great gift of being filled by You? Fill me with the renewable resource of Your power to do God's work. Amen.

Wake Up!

Awake, sleeper, and arise from the dead,
and Christ will shine on you.

EPHESIANS 5:14

I n the morning, whether by the sound of an alarm, the gentle touch of a spouse, or the bark of a hungry dog, we're awakened to let us know it's time to get going. It's time to wake up.

In his letter to the church of Ephesus, Paul was sounding the alarm to rouse— even jolt—them out of ongoing slumber and wake them up to the new spiritual reality in which they lived. The Christians at Ephesus lived in a society that was anti-God. Its people didn't operate according to divine guidelines.

To their credit and that of the Lord, this group of believers had made the radical choice to trust in Christ for salvation. They had set out on a unique pathway to become transformed. But unfortunately, they fell into a spiritual stupor as the pagan culture numbed their passion and swayed their choices.

So Paul keeps pointing them to the understanding that they aren't to function from a place on earth; they're to operate from heavenly places. He's trying to refocus them on the spiritual realm as their source so they will live with and make decisions from a kingdom mindset.

Far too many believers today are spiritually asleep. They're in a daze from drinking in the secular world instead of the Holy Spirit. Their senses and convictions are dulled by the stories, intrigues, and drama of an ungodly culture.

We need Paul's command today. We must hear the alarm clock of heaven, or we will be ineffective at impacting the world for God and for good. God desires to work through us for the betterment of others and the advancement of His kingdom agenda on earth. It's time for us to emerge from the darkness and have the light of Christ shining on us. It's time to wake up.

———

Holy Spirit, forgive me for becoming passive. I want to be passionate about the light of Christ. Thank You for waking me up to a kingdom mindset. Amen.

What Are You Full Of?

Jesus, full of the Holy Spirit, returned from the Jordan and
was led around by the Spirit in the wilderness for forty days,
being tempted by the devil. And He ate nothing during those
days, and when they had ended, He became hungry.

LUKE 4:1-2

It's not every day that a pastor encourages you to live under the influence, but I hope today's devotional inspires you to experience a life lived under the dominating influence of the Holy Spirit.

This can happen only when you allow the Spirit to completely fill you. Just like one sip of wine would have no impact on a person's behavior, a sip of the Spirit here or there won't either. You must be filled.

In today's passage, Luke references Jesus being "full" of the Holy Spirit, indicating He was "overwhelmed" by His presence. He was heavily influenced by the Spirit to the degree that He even allowed the Spirit to lead Him into the wilderness to face the devil.

Whenever you're full of something, that something controls you. Maybe you're full of sorrow, a condition Jesus attributed to His disciples in John 16:6. They were sad because He said He was leaving them, and that sadness was ruling their decisions. Or perhaps you're full of rage just as Luke tells us people in Jesus's own hometown of Nazareth were when anger at His teaching had consumed them so much that they literally wanted to throw Him off the edge of a cliff (Luke 4:28-29).

In other words, to be "full" of something means releasing control to that something or to someone. So much damage can be done when we surrender to the wrong things. But God wants to influence you in ways that will bring about good, not destruction. That's why He made His Spirit available to you—so you can be filled with the Spirit to such a degree that the Spirit directs your paths.

———

Holy Spirit, I've filled up on unimportant things. Release me from the emotions and choices that take up spiritual space that should be flowing with Your love and power. Amen.

Influence by the Spirit

Let the word of Christ richly dwell within you, with all wisdom
teaching and admonishing one another with psalms and hymns and
spiritual songs, singing with thankfulness in your hearts to God.

COLOSSIANS 3:16

Filled with the Spirit, your views and standards ought to be different. Your words definitely ought to be different. Even your courage to carry out God's will ought to be different.

In Paul's letters, he often reminds believers that we have a participatory role in the work of God in our lives. We must consistently minister to God as well as to others from a good heart. He also emphasizes gratitude as an atmosphere-creator for allowing the Spirit to fill us.

You can't be full of the Spirit if you're full of yourself, sin, or resistance. You can't be full of the Spirit if you choose to give your predominant focus to a culture's priorities and practices. The Holy Spirit will fill you only to the degree that you make space for Him to do so. Making space involves surrendering to Jesus Christ and yielding your life to Him on a continual basis while emptying yourself of anything else.

Let's go back to the comparison between the wine of alcohol and the wine of the Spirit. The phrase *social drinker* references someone who drinks at social events just to fit in, not to get drunk. Our culture also has *social Christians*. These individuals sip the Spirit in order to look the part and fit in. They sip a prayer here or there. But they don't want anything to do with being filled to the full by the Spirit of God. They want to keep their own control.

But sipping the Spirit will never give you access to His full power. Only when we live a courageous life of ministry—singing songs to God and to others, reading His Word, surrendering to the Word of Christ, and talking about Him to others—have we positioned ourselves to be filled, sated, and influenced by the Holy Spirit.

———

Holy Spirit, help me recognize when I'm being a social Christian instead of a surrendered believer. Influence me so that I am a godly influence in the world. Amen.

EXPERIENCE *the Wine*

FOCUS SCRIPTURE

Men of Judea and all you who live in Jerusalem, let this be known to you and give heed to my words. For these men are not drunk, as you suppose, for it is only the third hour of the day; but this is what was spoken of through the prophet Joel: "And it shall be in the last days," God says, "that I will pour forth of My Spirit on all mankind" (Acts 2:14-17).

When have you felt under the influence of the Holy Spirit?

_____

_____

_____

FOR REFLECTION

Describe a time you encountered the Holy Spirit as the Wine.

_____

_____

_____

Which characteristic of the Wine draws you closer to God? Why?

_____

_____

_____

Which message from the devotions this week did you most need—and why?

_____

_____

_____

PERSONAL PRAYER

I praise You, Spirit, as the Wine, for...

_____

_____

_____

Forgive me, Spirit, as the Wine, when I...

_____

_____

_____

I'm grateful to You, Spirit, as the Wine, for...

_____

_____

_____

Spirit, as the Wine, today I need Your help to...

_____

_____

_____

In its original language, the Bible's term for "be filled" when talking about the Holy Spirit is a passive, present plural imperative. That means it's a command, not a suggestion. God isn't asking you to consider being filled. Nor is He recommending that you be filled. Paul, under the guidance of the Spirit in writing "be filled with the Spirit" (Ephesians 5:18), is *commanding* that you be filled.

Bear the Fruit

The fruit of the Spirit is love, joy, peace, patience, kindness, goodness, faithfulness, gentleness, self-control; against such things there is no law. Now those who belong to Christ Jesus have crucified the flesh with its passions and desires.

GALATIANS 5:22-24

This name, the Fruit, representing the person and work of the Holy Spirit, is key to helping each of us unlock our greatest potential for Christ. The Spirit's fruit is His ability to assist believers in bearing *their* fruit.

In today's passage from Galatians, Paul is talking about the Spirit as a fruit-bearing tree allowing believers to maximize their spiritual productivity and Christ-like character. He points out how the believers ought to be treating one another and introduces them to the fruit of the Spirit.

Friend, this isn't a message to look at as part of biblical history. This is a timely, vital message for us today about how we're to relate to one another—by reflecting the Holy Spirit's person and work within us. Rather than being destructive toward one another, we are to be healing agents for good. Rather than bickering, blaming, and backstabbing in the body of Christ, we are to reflect love, joy, peace, patience, kindness, goodness, faithfulness, gentleness, and self-control. Only the Spirit can address and rectify the depth of division that has crept into Christian circles today.

A battle between the flesh and the Spirit goes on within us. The flesh is that desire in you to please yourself independently of God. In other words, you want to please yourself in a way that goes outside God's prescribed means. Yet the Spirit is the presence of Christ within each of us that stirs a desire to please God even more than we aim to please ourselves.

The flesh doesn't need to have power over you. Increase the influence of the Spirit in your life, and you will bear the fruit of the Spirit. Then you can unlock and live out your potential for Christ. You can show up and treat others in a Christ-like way.

Holy Spirit, I seek Your encouragement to bear the fruit of the Spirit. When my flesh battles the fruit, remind me of the witness my faithfulness can have. Amen.

You Can't Fix the Flesh

You foolish Galatians, who has bewitched you, before whose eyes
Jesus Christ was publicly portrayed as crucified? This is the only
thing I want to find out from you: did you receive the Spirit by the
works of the Law, or by hearing with faith? Are you so foolish? Having
begun by the Spirit, are you now being perfected by the flesh?

GALATIANS 3:1-3

People spend an inordinate amount of money on counseling and all kinds of therapies to try to make the flesh less fleshy. And while I believe counseling and therapy are important, the bottom line is always about whether the Spirit is allowed to dominate over the flesh. Without this understanding, we have to settle for flesh management instead of spiritual transformation.

Paul let the Galatians know they'd been duped by flesh-management programs, sermons, and more. They'd bought into the lie far too many preachers promote today—that everyone's job is to fix their own flesh. But the goal of the Christian life is never to fix the flesh. And the goal of the Holy Spirit is to override the flesh.

Let's use an example common in today's body-focused culture. Someone who's weight training is trying to lose fat and build muscle, but they can't turn fat into muscle. Yet countless people have still invested in "get fit quick" schemes promising this kind of miracle even though it contradicts anatomy and physiology. Fat is fat. And muscle is muscle. Period.

Similarly, the flesh and the Spirit are each distinct. You're born with the flesh, but you won't get rid of it by trying to turn it into the Spirit. You can only reduce the flesh's influence while simultaneously strengthening the Spirit's influence in your life. You reduce the power of the flesh as you grow in walking in the Spirit.

Paul doesn't say you'll no longer have the desires of the flesh. He says you will no longer carry out those desires. If you've been striving to fix your flesh, it's time to turn your inner work toward true transformation by allowing the person and work of the Spirit to be made manifest in your life.

———

Holy Spirit, forgive me for returning to the futile work of trying to fix the flesh when I have Your power within to override it. Transform me, Lord. Amen.

The Law of Love

You were called to freedom, brethren; only do not turn your freedom
into an opportunity for the flesh, but through love serve one another.
For the whole Law is fulfilled in one word, in the statement, "You
shall love your neighbor as yourself." But if you bite and devour one
another, take care that you are not consumed by one another.

GALATIANS 5:13-15

As a boy, one of my favorite family traditions was eating steamed crabs. Whenever my father could afford it, he would bring live crabs home on Friday. Now, when crabs are in a pot of boiling water, a few of them will try to climb out. But the other crabs grab at the runaways as they, too, try to get out. Their claws destroy one another, which keeps them all in the same situation of destruction.

Whether this story made you hungry or sad for the crabs, stick with me.

In Galatians, Paul voiced his concern that the Christians were acting more like crabs than like believers. They were destroying one another rather than serving, helping, and loving one another. We need this same talking-to. The problems prevalent today—cultural, racial, political, or any other—have induced an atmosphere of vitriolic hate.

While this reality may be true for the world as a general rule, it ought not be normative among the people of God. God doesn't want us clamoring, clawing, and yanking one another down in our desperation to lift ourselves up. Rather, He wants us all to experience biblical freedom, so we can maximize our spiritual calling and potential.

When you realize the flesh will always be the flesh, you can trust that which is a greater law. The law of love as manifested in the law of the Spirit thus overrides the flesh's control over you so the Spirit can produce His fruit in your life.

Today, rest in the truth that you are called to freedom, and in the law of love and the Spirit, you will bear the fruit to lift up others rather than claw them down.

———

Holy Spirit, convict me when I bring others down. I want to stop sowing seeds of controversy so I can sow seeds of Your fruit to encourage healing and hope in others. Amen.

Walk Until You Soar

I say, walk by the Spirit, and you will not carry out the desire
of the flesh. For the flesh sets its desire against the Spirit, and
the Spirit against the flesh; for these are in opposition to one
another, so that you may not do the things that you please. But
if you are led by the Spirit, you are not under the Law.

GALATIANS 5:16-18

To understand the spiritual laws of love and the Spirit, let's first look at a couple of physical laws. The law of gravity is a nonnegotiable law. What goes up must come down. Yet we can fly on an airplane and not come crashing down. Why? Because another law supersedes the law of gravity—the law of aerodynamics. It says when you move at a certain speed given the right amount of thrust, you don't cancel out gravity. But you do override it.

The Spirit acts in much the same way this law of aerodynamics acts toward the law of gravity. While there's a law of sin that wages war, the law of the Spirit can override it, enabling us to rise above our sin. The solution to every relational issue, internal conflict, addiction, or any sin issue you face is found in learning to walk in the Spirit.

Walking is a great analogy because it gives us three ways to live in the Spirit—destination, dependency, and dedication. When you walk in the Spirit, you are to:

- Pursue the destinations of spiritual maturity, kingdom impact, and God's will.

- Surrender dependency on yourself and depend on God to get you where you need to go.

- Be dedicated to take steps of faith toward God's will.

The Holy Spirit will help you learn to walk spiritually, override the flesh, and take step after step until you're uplifted and soaring in the power of God.

———

Holy Spirit, I feel the gravity of the world. May Your power override this pull and help me pursue God's will in Your strength. Amen.

EXPERIENCE *the Fruit*

FOCUS SCRIPTURE

Those who are according to the flesh set their minds on the things of the flesh, but those who are according to the Spirit, the things of the Spirit (Romans 8:5).

What are two ways you can set your mind on the Spirit this week?

_____

_____

_____

FOR REFLECTION

Describe a time you encountered the Holy Spirit as the Fruit.

_____

_____

_____

Which characteristic of the Fruit draws you closer to God?

_____

_____

_____

Which message from the devotions this week did you most need—and why?

_____

_____

_____

PERSONAL PRAYER

I praise You, Spirit, as the Fruit, for...

_____

_____

_____

Forgive me, Spirit, as the Fruit, when I...

_____

_____

_____

I'm grateful to You, Spirit, as the Fruit, for...

_____

_____

_____

Spirit, as the Fruit, today I need Your help to...

_____

_____

_____

Paul speaks from experience when he writes to the church at Galatia. In the book of Romans, he shares his personal struggle with his flesh (chapter 7). He doesn't share what the specific fleshy thing he's wrestling with is, but he lets us know it's difficult to overcome. He wrestled with it until he came to this conclusion: "There is now no condemnation for those who are in Christ Jesus. For the law of the Spirit of life in Christ Jesus has set you free from the law of sin and of death" (Romans 8:1-2).

INTERCESSOR

Understanding Pain

Having the first fruits of the Spirit, even we ourselves groan within ourselves, waiting eagerly for our adoption as sons, the redemption of our body. For in hope we have been saved, but hope that is seen is not hope; for who hopes for what he already sees? But if we hope for what we do not see, with perseverance we wait eagerly for it.

ROMANS 8:23-25

Life hurts. And as I've become all too familiar with recently, at times circumstances and loss affect you to such a degree that all you can do is groan. Do you know what it's like to run out of words to explain what you're going through or to pray? At one point or another, most of us have. Which is why God has given us this most powerful and needed character attribute and role of the Holy Spirit: Intercessor.

An intercessor appeals to someone on behalf of a situation or another person. Paul tells us we have an intercessor when life causes us to groan. We have a representative when we face suffering. In short, we have hope.

He begins by telling us that suffering is literally part of the created order. He relates the groaning of childbirth to the groaning of earth itself through creation. This gives us a theological and spiritual way to understand earthquakes, hurricanes, and other natural disasters that seem to come out of nowhere, including a pandemic caused by a virus. These are the groanings of the globe.

Suffering is a reminder to each of us that this life and this world are not all there is. So when you're groaning within the depths of your soul like a woman groans for her deliverance in childbirth, that pain exists to produce a spiritual shift. This is why God allows reminders that will force us toward a spiritual perspective to enter into our existence. And you and I are to allow the groanings to recalibrate our thinking, to not only see the pain but to understand the purpose.

Holy Spirit, my suffering is giving birth to something new, because I surrender my pain to You and You intercede on my behalf. You know the groanings of my soul. Amen.

Hope in God

We had the sentence of death within ourselves so that we
would not trust in ourselves, but in God who raises the
dead; who delivered us from so great a peril of death, and
will deliver us, He on whom we have set our hope.

2 CORINTHIANS 1:9-10

Life and peace are found only when you understand the spiritual nature of the soul you've been blessed to embody in human form.

The mind set on the flesh focuses on the human limitations of this life. It functions from the viewpoint of a funeral home. It's about death. Whether that's the death of dreams, hopes, desires, or even our physical realities, this world offers only what remains in this world.

The mind set on the Spirit is life and peace. It's akin to walking out of a funeral home on a sunny day and hearing the birds chirp, knowing that the spiritual realm goes beyond the limits of our senses. But it's easy to forget the spiritual when the pain of the physical dominates our psyche, and that's why Paul reminds us of the Intercessor. Paul knew great pain and affliction.

In today's verses, Paul references a "sentence of death," which is just another way to say he was emotionally suicidal. When death looks brighter than life, a person is operating from a suicidal standpoint. Even spiritual people can wish to be set free from the confines of this world.

I hope Paul's transparency will give you courage and comfort. Our hardships, like his did for Paul, offer us a spiritual perspective. We discover this valuable lesson: It's always better to hope in God than to trust in yourself.

This lesson sounds so simple. To actually live in alignment with it as truth, however, is a lot more difficult for all of us. When you understand this truth, it changes the decisions you make, and it changes your emotions within those decisions. It changes your prayer life. It changes where you place your trust and hope. It changes everything.

———

Holy Spirit, I've leaned into spiritual death during seasons of discouragement. Help me place my hope in You each day so the peace of the Intercessor anchors me. Amen.

Translator of the Heart

In the same way the Spirit also helps our weakness; for we do
not know how to pray as we should, but the Spirit Himself
intercedes for us with groanings too deep for words; and He who
searches the hearts knows what the mind of the Spirit is, because
He intercedes for the saints according to the will of God.

ROMANS 8:26-27

When you are in a foreign country and don't know the language, you need either an interpreter or an interpretation app on your phone. You need someone or something to help you communicate. The Holy Spirit serves in this capacity for us since we don't know how to speak the language of heaven—and sometimes even when we have difficulty expressing our deepest needs in the languages on earth. The Spirit can hear our spirit within when we don't have the words to express what we're feeling.

Anytime you're trying to reach God in the midst of your pain, that pain may distort your thinking. You may not know what to ask for in accordance with God's will. This is because you're just trying to address the pain and remove it, fix it, or change it. But the prayers answered are those given in alignment with God's will. As 1 John 5:14-15 says, "This is the confidence which we have before Him, that, if we ask anything according to His will, He hears us. And if we know that He hears us in whatever we ask, we know that we have the requests which we have asked from Him."

The Holy Spirit will take our desires and clarify our requests so they align with God's will as much as possible.

When the pain is so deep that you can't even get words out, or all you can do is cry because the hurt is like a hurricane within, the Holy Spirit is there to help you. Paul tells us that's when He intercedes on our behalf with His own groanings too deep for words. He goes to God on our behalf to seek our relief and the way out of the depths of pain that engulf us.

———

Holy Spirit, I don't always understand what I need! Thank You for being the translator of my hurts and hopes so the Father can discern my deepest wounds and needs. Amen.

Transformed in the Waiting

We know that God causes all things to work together for good
to those who love God, to those who are called according
to His purpose. For those whom He foreknew, He also
predestined to become conformed to the image of His Son, so
that He would be the firstborn among many brethren.

ROMANS 8:28-29

Let's be honest. Isn't instant relief what we're really hoping for when we pray? We pray as though we're placing an order for relief with Amazon's same-day service. We don't want it delivered next week or even tomorrow. But we won't get the relief we need until we learn how to pray according to God's will. And the Holy Spirit's role is to help us conform to God's will. This is often done through a doctrine called providence—the mysterious way God intercedes and interconnects things in order to unite them for His sovereign purpose.

There's a difference between God's providence and His miracles. A miracle is when God transcends His laws He built into creation. But providence is when God works within His natural laws to stitch things together in order to weave them into the place of alignment with His will.

Now, in order for you to see His providential work in your life, you must have a heart that's in love with Him. And to love God is to passionately pursue His glory. It's stating *Not my will but Your will be done* and meaning it with all of your heart.

If God is stretching you, pressing you, and allowing all manner of difficulty to happen to you—and you love Him—then be assured that He's seeking to conform you to Christ. He wants to develop something in you by shifting things outside of you in order to transform you.

Friend, if you choose to love God and walk in His ways, you'll experience the Spirit's power of interceding on your behalf. But it starts with you. It starts with your heart. Your mind. Your will. The Spirit is waiting. He longs to intercede for you, if you will simply allow Him to do what He does best.

———

Holy Spirit, in times of waiting, the doubts creep in, and my insecurities rise. May I trust that You are shaping me into a new creation. Amen.

EXPERIENCE *the Intercessor*

FOCUS SCRIPTURE

The mind set on the flesh is death, but the mind set on the Spirit is life and peace (Romans 8:6).

Have you ever felt like you were experiencing spiritual death? How did the Intercessor intervene?

_____

_____

_____

FOR REFLECTION

Describe a time you encountered the Holy Spirit as the Intercessor.

_____

_____

_____

Which characteristic of the Intercessor draws you closer to God? Why?

_____

_____

_____

Which message from the devotions this week did you most need—and why?

_____

_____

_____

PERSONAL PRAYER

I praise You, Spirit, as the Intercessor, for...

_____

_____

_____

Forgive me, Spirit, as the Intercessor, when I...

_____

_____

_____

I'm grateful to You, Spirit, as the Intercessor, for...

_____

_____

_____

Spirit, as the Intercessor, today I need Your help to...

_____

_____

_____

God wants to hear what our heart is saying when we cry out to Him. Isaiah 29:13 emphasizes this truth for us: "Then the Lord said, 'Because this people draw near with their words and honor Me with their lip service, but they remove their hearts far from Me, and their reverence for Me consists of tradition learned by rote...'" God can hear the expressions of your spirit through the Holy Spirit, who lives to intercede on your behalf.

Relief Is Near

In Him, you also, after listening to the message of truth, the gospel of your salvation—having also believed, you were sealed in Him with the Holy Spirit of promise, who is given as a pledge of our inheritance, with a view to the redemption of God's own possession, to the praise of His glory.

EPHESIANS 1:13-14

Do you know the advertisement jingle "Plop, plop, fizz, fizz—oh, what a relief it is!"? That's from Alka Seltzer commercials where the medicinal tablets are dropped into water and transformation occurs. What was once water turns into an empowered liquid able to bring relief for indigestion. It's the indwelling of the tablets in the water that brings about the change.

The tablets are what they are even without being in the water. But when they indwell the water, they turn into a more viable solution to the problem.

Every believer who's trusted Jesus Christ has plop, plop, fizz, fizz relief because they possess the Holy Spirit. The Holy Spirit is a new resident in an old house. This old house of our humanity, which over time fades away, has now been indwelt with the person of the Spirit. The third member of the Trinity was dropped into your spirit in order to operate as a permanent part of your humanity from then on. His presence brings relief to life's disturbances and pains.

The Seal is the name for the Holy Spirit that emphasizes His role of indwelling. Just as the tablets added to the water become a permanent portion of that water, so does the Holy Spirit become a permanent resident in each of us when we're saved.

The advancement of God's kingdom agenda on earth is all about promoting the glory of God. The Holy Spirit's permanent presence within you enables you to bring greater glory to God as you receive His relief when you need it and seek Him as your source of comfort daily.

———

Holy Spirit, You indwell my house of humanity. I seek Your comfort and relief in my life right now. I praise God for providing Your soothing presence within me. Amen.

You Can't Save Yourself

You have been bought with a price: therefore glorify God in your body.

1 CORINTHIANS 6:20

I'm always surprised when a believer says they're worried about losing their salvation. If you've ever had this fear, friend, I have good news for you: The sealing presence of the Spirit preserves your salvation. Once you've trusted in Jesus Christ, you've been born into the family of God and sealed with the Spirit. The name "the Seal" guarantees your security. You can't lose that spiritual connection or undo your salvation.

This name for the Holy Spirit also indicates ownership. In our contemporary life, we establish both authenticity and ownership with a seal. If we buy a car, we have the title sealed to identify the ownership as legitimate. As children of the King, we've been bought with the high price of the atonement of Jesus and thus sealed under the ownership of God.

When believers think they own their lives, they get lost on the pathway. We own nothing. That's why the Bible calls us stewards. We're blessed to use that which God provides, but we're to use it as stewards or managers. We're to do so under the guidance of the true Owner, God Himself.

Last, the Seal indicates authorization. When Jesus Christ saved you and gave you the Holy Spirit, He gave you divine authorization to utilize the Spirit on your behalf. The question to ask yourself is this: *Have I surrendered ownership to the Lord Jesus Christ so that the Spirit of God can do what He wants to do in my life?* If you have surrendered, rest in the fullness of your salvation—the security, ownership, and authorization of the Seal—by tapping into and living from all of the benefits of the Spirit. If you haven't surrendered, then the bigger question is this: What are you waiting for?

———

Holy Spirit, if I worry about my salvation, I'm not trusting the true source of that gift! I'm grateful that the Seal has locked in my salvation forever. Amen.

Maximize the Spirit

*I pray that the eyes of your heart may be enlightened, so that
you will know what is the hope of His calling, what are the riches
of the glory of His inheritance in the saints, and what is the
surpassing greatness of His power toward us who believe.*

EPHESIANS 1:18-19

Maximizing the Holy Spirit's role in your life equates to maximizing your life. Whenever the Holy Spirit is free to fully work both in and through you, you become empowered to live out your purpose and calling. And in doing these things, you find true satisfaction and joy.

The power and enlightenment of the Seal that Paul writes about is not out of reach or out of your spiritual league. God works experientially in your life through the indwelling of the Holy Spirit. The Seal enlightens you and informs your human spirit through the revelation and knowledge of Him. But to perceive things spiritually and apply God's truth to that which you perceive, you must receive this gift and access it by acknowledging and living according to the ownership and authority of God over you.

When you do, you're released to experience more of God's reality. You begin to see the things around you more clearly. You'll experience Him showing up for you in ways you never anticipated. The decisions you need to make will make sense. The courage required of you to walk by faith will be infused in you. You will gain clarity and conviction to live out the calling God has in store for your life. You will be able to discern whether something is truly good for you or actually bad for you. You'll know whether God brought something to you all tied up with a nice bow or if Satan, the master deceiver, did.

The Holy Spirit will enable and empower you to know the hope of your calling. Don't miss out on this gift of God. Discover how to walk according to the illumination of spiritual eyes, and you'll discover a life you only dreamed of before.

———

Holy Spirit, You give me so much. Reveal to me the ways I'm not accessing Your power and clarity. Give me the hope of Your calling, and let it guide me always. Amen.

It's Your Choice

He made known His ways to Moses, His acts to the sons of Israel.

PSALM 103:7

Which do you look at—God's ways or His acts? Moses saw God's ways. He saw who God is. Israel only saw what God did. They missed the deeper understanding of the Lord's why and how behind His ways.

How you see and experience God is up to you. Do you want to sit on the sidelines and watch what He does for other people? Or do you want to walk up the mountain to experience Him, like Moses did, face-to-face? God will never force you to walk according to His ways. But He will enable you to do so through the sealing of the Holy Spirit. What you do with His gift is entirely up to you.

We are given free will. If we want to remain autonomous, God gives us that choice. But if we do make that choice, we'll also be choosing to live life apart from spiritual enlightenment. Our choices and emotions will no doubt reflect this reality. Only when we allow all of the elements of the seal of the Holy Spirit to be fully expressed in our life will we tap into all of the benefits the Spirit is designed to supply.

You and I belong to Jesus Christ, and He has a good plan for our lives. But we'll experience this plan only when we choose to allow the Holy Spirit to fully express Himself inside our lives. Not only are we sealed for eternity by the power of the Spirit within, but when we sync with the Holy Spirit in our everyday activities and thoughts, we're enabled to live out the full manifestation of our calling and purpose on earth. The choice is ours.

———

Holy Spirit, I want to see God face-to-face. I want to experience Him fully. May the Seal be expressed through my soul and being with great force. Amen.

EXPERIENCE *the Seal*

FOCUS SCRIPTURE

Who will separate us from the love of Christ?...For I am convinced that neither death, nor life, nor angels, nor principalities, nor things present, nor things to come, nor powers, nor height, nor depth, nor any other created thing, will be able to separate us from the love of God, which is in Christ Jesus our Lord (Romans 8:35, 38-39).

Express how you feel knowing that nothing can separate you from the love of God and your salvation.

_____

_____

_____

FOR REFLECTION

Describe a time you encountered the Holy Spirit as the Seal.

_____

_____

_____

Which characteristic of the Seal draws you closer to God? Why?

_____

_____

_____

Which message from the devotions this week did you most need—and why?

_____

_____

_____

PERSONAL PRAYER

I praise You, Spirit, as the Seal, for...

_____

_____

_____

Forgive me, Spirit, as the Seal, when I...

_____

_____

_____

I'm grateful to You, Spirit, as the Seal, for...

_____

_____

_____

Spirit, as the Seal, today I need Your help to...

_____

_____

_____

As we see in the Scripture below, Paul championed believers to find security in the Seal of the Spirit so they could experience God fully. This is my hope for you too.

For this reason I too, having heard of the faith in the Lord Jesus which exists among you and your love for all the saints, do not cease giving thanks for you, while making mention of you in my prayers; that the God of our Lord Jesus Christ, the Father of glory, may give to you a spirit of wisdom and of revelation in the knowledge of Him (Ephesians 1:15-17).

How We Can Breathe

The LORD God formed man of dust from the ground, and breathed
into his nostrils the breath of life; and man became a living being.

GENESIS 2:7

We became all too familiar with the phrase *I can't breathe* in 2020. While the words came literally attached to the deaths of Eric Garner and George Floyd, the refrain itself arose to symbolically describe the historical oppression of a group of people. Shirts, posters, hats, chants—you name it—held up this phrase over and over again for the world to see. It took on its own meaning as it grew into a worldwide movement.

What's more, as the COVID-19 pandemic continued to display its ugly claws on society's stage, many more people lost their lives through their inability to breathe. The struggle for breath was a challenge so many faced—and on so many levels.

We all know how serious these words are. The inability to breathe means life is in jeopardy. Conversely, the ability to breathe means we're able to take in life and are free to live. Breath matters. It matters for good, and it's terribly detrimental when the ability to breathe is lost. That's why this name for the Holy Spirit is so important. The Bible refers to the Spirit as the Breath. He is literally the oxygen of God.

God used the Spirit as His breath hovering over creation and bringing life out of chaos in the Genesis 1 story of creation. And in today's verse we read that He breathed life into Adam. Spiritual life and death in the physical realm are tied to our relationship with the Holy Spirit because that's the relationship we have to breathe.

The degree to which you breathe in the Holy Spirit is the degree to which you're able to experience the life and presence of God. It's also the degree to which you experience hope in the midst of the hopelessness. Honor the Breath with gratitude today.

———

Holy Spirit, I need Your life-giving breath. I feel my energy leaving me. I feel the turmoil and chaos around me. Help me pause and take in the peace of Your presence. Amen.

Peace Be with You

The disciples then rejoiced when they saw the Lord. So Jesus
said to them again, "Peace be with you; as the Father has sent
Me, I also send you." And when He had said this, He breathed
on them and said to them, "Receive the Holy Spirit."

JOHN 20:20-22

Has anyone ever instructed you to "Just breathe" when you were afraid? After Jesus had been crucified, the disciples were huddled together in a locked room, afraid that those who killed Him would come for them. So when Jesus comes to them in that room after His resurrection, He sees their terror. Out of love, He responds with His version of "Just breathe," which was "Peace be with you." Then He transferred the Holy Spirit to the disciples through His breath. And when He did that, they breathed in the Spirit.

Today there is a lot to fear in our world. Deadly viruses. Violence. Racial strife. The next storm. And when we're holding our breath out of fear or reluctant to step outside the home of our comfort zones, Jesus does for us what He did for the disciples. When we let Him in, He comes through the door of our heart and brings us the peace of His presence and the breath of the Holy Spirit.

Jesus knew we would need the Spirit of life breathed into our hearts, calming us from fear and uniting us with the Holy Spirit for our faith journey. This connection is reinforced when we engage with the Word of God, which gives life.

In 2 Timothy 3:16, the Bible says "All Scripture is inspired by God." The Greek word in that passage is *theopneustos,* which means "to breathe out." This lets us know that Scripture is the Holy Spirit. It's the inspired Spirit of God in print.

Friend, when you're aligned with the Holy Spirit, and the Word of God is living within you through the breath of the Spirit, the peace of God will manifest in your life and in your circumstances.

Holy Spirit, stories of Jesus's love fill me with peace. After making the ultimate sacrifice, He chose to encourage the disciples. He does the same for me. Amen.

Spiritual Oxygen

The Spirit of God has made me,
and the breath of the Almighty gives me life.

JOB 33:4

One of the problems that runs rampant in our Christian culture today is a lack of Holy Spirit oxygen. Christians are not breathing in the Holy Spirit, and so they have no spiritual oxygen circulating in them. Just as the physical body begins to break down without oxygen, the spiritual life does as well. The latter can show up in anxiety, depression, irritability, vitriol, despondency, or an incessant searching for hedonistic pleasures. We can't expect to thrive without the oxygen of the Spirit.

We, like Dr. Frankenstein's monster, may have the anatomy of a human being, but without a fully healthy soul we are anything but alive. For too many people, this results in monstrous behavior in attitudes and actions, character and conduct, because they have access to the body but without the life to guide it to its proper use.

God is the life within us. Psalm 104:30 tells us how God makes us alive: "You send forth Your Spirit, they are created; and You renew the face of the ground." We are alive when the Spirit's breath is within us. Without it, we are merely men and women in bodies.

The Spirit is the life-Source to each of us as believers, but you and I have choice and free will. We must choose to inhale deeply and frequently in order to receive and experience the full benefit of the breath. He infuses you with the oxygen of His life so you can make a spiritual impact as you follow Him and demonstrate to a watching world what living by faith truly means. Friend, accessing and maximizing the spiritual life happens only when we stay tied to the ongoing flow of the Spirit. If your spiritual life is not producing fruit, commit to deeply inhaling the Breath daily.

Holy Spirit, when You arise in me as the Breath, the fear I've been holding starts to fade. I pause to remember You as the source of life and goodness and grace. Amen.

Connected to the Spirit

If we live by the Spirit, let us also walk by the Spirit.

GALATIANS 5:25

When you breathe, do you inhale and hold it? Do you take one breath and then go about your business for the day? Or do you breathe, let the breath out; breathe again, let the breath out again; and so forth all day long? Of course you do the latter. It's the way we've been designed. In fact, we don't even need to think about it. Most of us breathe without thinking. We breathe without effort. That's how God wants our relationship to be when we rely on the Holy Spirit for the spiritual oxygen we need.

We are to breathe in concert with the Spirit so that it becomes second nature to us. We are to reflect His thoughts in our hearts and minds without having to make any effort to do so. We are to walk so closely with Him that His breath is a natural extension of our own. His voice is a natural part of our own. His leading is naturally taken into consideration in every decision we make. We shouldn't have to think too hard to consult the Spirit, because when He's an ongoing part of our everyday lives, He's so near that He's advising and guiding us without our even having to ask Him to.

When we walk in step with the Spirit and breathe in unison with Him, we have everything we need to overcome all that comes at us. God's Spirit gives us the power we need to overcome anything. Politicians and revolutionaries don't have the last say. Even your boss doesn't have the last say. It is God who speaks in such a way that creation listens. It is God who supplies all you need to live your life to the fullest and who opens the doors you don't even know to knock on.

———

Holy Spirit, I want my breath, thoughts, pace, and hope to move in unison with You. You inspire life in and through me. Thank You, breath of God. Amen.

EXPERIENCE *the Breath*

FOCUS SCRIPTURE

The hand of the LORD was upon me, and He brought me out by the Spirit of the LORD and set me down in the middle of the valley; and it was full of bones... He said to me, "Prophesy over these bones and say to them, 'O dry bones, hear the word of the LORD.' Thus says the Lord GOD to these bones, 'Behold, I will cause breath to enter you that you may come to life. I will put sinews on you, make flesh grow back on you, cover you with skin and put breath in you that you may come alive; and you will know that I am the LORD'" (Ezekiel 37:1, 4-6).

In what ways are you experiencing the weariness of your old bones and old mindset?

_____

_____

_____

FOR REFLECTION

Describe a time you encountered the Holy Spirit as the Breath.

_____

_____

Which characteristic of the Breath draws you closer to God? Why?

_____

_____

Which message from the devotions this week did you most need—and why?

_____

_____

_____

PERSONAL PRAYER

I praise You, Spirit, as the Breath, for…

_____

_____

_____

Forgive me, Spirit, as the Breath, when I…

_____

_____

_____

I'm grateful to You, Spirit, as the Breath, for…

_____

_____

_____

Spirit, as the Breath, today I need Your help to…

_____

_____

_____

The New Testament word for the Spirit here is *pneuma*. In fact, that's where we get our contemporary English term *pneumonia*. As you can see, we have directly tied a word indicating a failure or difficulty to breathe due to sickness to the original term, which spoke of the Spirit. The Hebrew word in the Old Testament for the breath of God, which is the Spirit of God, is *ruach*. This appears in Genesis 2:7 when God breathes life into Adam.

Invisible Strength

He said to them, "It is not for you to know times or epochs which the Father has fixed by His own authority; but you will receive power when the Holy Spirit has come upon you; and you shall be My witnesses both in Jerusalem, and in all Judea and Samaria, and even to the remotest part of the earth."

ACTS 1:7-8

You don't have to see something for it to provide immense benefit to your life. None of us can see electricity, yet electricity empowers much of what we do. None of us see the Holy Spirit, yet the Holy Spirit gives life to all we do.

This name for the Holy Spirit—the Power—describes an attribute of His that's important for us to understand and live into. We discover it in the book of Acts, at the conclusion of the 40-day window between Jesus's resurrection and His ascension. During these last moments, He met with His followers to talk about what would happen when He left.

The disciples wanted to know when Jesus would be returning to set up His kingdom, and He told them it was not for them to know. But He did want them to know that even though He was leaving them in His physical presence, He was still going to share His power with them. When He ascended into heaven, He'd leave behind the person of the Holy Spirit, who would transfer His spiritual power both to them and to each of us. His followers were to be vested with the power to carry out God's kingdom agenda while on earth.

When Jesus did that, through the Holy Spirit, He supplied us with kingdom electricity to bring about God's overarching goal in history.

This attribute of power is one of the most misunderstood and underutilized aspects of the Holy Spirit. The Holy Spirit is a powerful member of the Trinity. He takes from God the power that is God's and delivers it to you and me so that the power of heaven is made available to us. Are you living from that power? Are you serving God in it?

———

Holy Spirit, my stubbornness keeps me from fully using the power available to me. Help me to live in Your strength. I need and want Your kingdom electricity. Amen.

Divine Dynamite

To Him who is able to do far more abundantly beyond all that we ask or think, according to the power that works within us, to Him be the glory in the church and in Christ Jesus to all generations forever and ever. Amen.

EPHESIANS 3:20-21

Have you ever been left on the side of the road because your car battery went dead? That happened to me once. I'll never forget standing there with my car's hood up. After a while, someone kind stopped and offered to jump-start my car. He took the jumper cables from his own car and hooked them up to mine in order to transfer power. I had the manual that explained what I needed to do, yet I couldn't revive my battery until someone transferred the power I needed.

The Bible contains all of the information we need in order to live our lives to the full. But if we're not properly hooked up to the Holy Spirit, it won't mean anything. We won't be able to go anywhere. Information without power is useless. The Holy Spirit must supply the power we need in order to enable us to use it.

Have you ever been spiritually stuck? In these times, you don't see any improvement or maturing process in your life. This is because you've been disconnected from the Holy Spirit's power. He still lives inside of you, but the cables that once connected you to His power—the cables of communion and abiding with Him—have come undone.

When Jesus ascended to heaven and left His followers on earth, He left us the *dunamis.* which is the power in the person of the Spirit. And the word *dunamis* is the word from which we derive our English word *dynamite.*

The Holy Spirit is not simply a trickling of power to give us a little boost. He contains so much power that Jesus described Him as dynamite. Through that power, God is able to do far more than you can imagine.

———

Holy Spirit, You are spiritual dynamite in a human world of fizzling sparklers. Fill me with all that comes with Your power. I want Your supernatural love, grace, and strength. Amen.

Brand-New Clothes

Behold, I am sending forth the promise of My Father upon you; but you
are to stay in the city until you are clothed with power from on high.

LUKE 24:49

If you want to take an even deeper look at the battery source every Christian has
been given, look at Acts 1:5: "John baptized with water, but you will be baptized
with the Holy Spirit not many days from now." The Greek word *baptizo* speaks of
something being identified. Here's an illustration: A woman wants to make a pink
dress for her daughter, so she takes some white cloth to a dye-maker. He dips the
cloth in pink dye, and now the cloth has been reidentified.

To be baptized is to reidentify yourself as a follower of Jesus Christ. Water
baptism is simply a visible modeling of spiritual baptism. Now, baptism doesn't
save you, as is evidenced by Jesus saying the thief on the cross next to Him was
saved though, obviously, he never had the opportunity to be baptized. The gospel saves you (1 Corinthians 15:1-2). But once you are saved, God expects you
to move into discipleship through your public identification with Jesus Christ.

In today's verse, Luke is warning the disciples not to go ahead and do the work
of the kingdom until the power of the Spirit comes upon them. Luke used the
word *clothed* to describe this. God expects us to wear Jesus Christ through the presence of the Spirit.

As Christians, we are to wear Christ's character, attributes, and qualities in such
a way that they publicly identify us as His followers. There should be no question
about to whom you belong or whose team you represent. Baptism indicates that
you are a visible, identifiable kingdom disciple. When you commit to this and
walk in the truth of what baptism represents, you will experience the Spirit's power.

---

*Holy Spirit, clothe me with the Power. Head to foot, and mind to heart to spirit, I want
to be immersed in You to show the world my identity as a Christ follower. Amen.*

Glorify the Giver

*If you then, being evil, know how to give good gifts
to your children, how much more will your heavenly
Father give the Holy Spirit to those who ask Him?*

LUKE 11:13

Now, this may be a shock to some believers, but making a big deal about us is not the Holy Spirit's goal. Neither is it the Holy Spirit's goal to make a big deal about Himself. The Holy Spirit's goal is to make a big deal about Jesus Christ. And our role on earth is to abide in Christ, to be identified with Jesus, and to advance His kingdom by glorifying Jesus Christ. When we make Him known in all we say and do, we accomplish that goal.

The word *glorify* means to put something on display. To glorify means to exclaim in a way that is unmistakable. The Holy Spirit will empower the amplification of Jesus Christ in your life. The intentional pursuit of Jesus is what turns on the ignition of the power of the Spirit in your life. And as this happens, you'll be infused with more power, more wisdom, and more strength in your life.

We make this too hard sometimes. We make "Holy Spirit hunting" our goal and complicate everything. Simply request the presence and power of the Holy Spirit in you on a continuous basis. Glorify Jesus, identify with Jesus, and abide in Jesus, and you will have the fullest expression of the Holy Spirit in your life any human being can. In fact, you'll have so much power that it will overflow naturally as you become His witness to others. You won't even have to try to be a witness for Jesus. Sharing Him and the gospel will come naturally to you. Living out the love of Jesus Christ will come naturally to you.

Life is complicated enough, so don't make your access to the Spirit complicated when it doesn't need to be. Come to the power of the Spirit and ask to be filled.

———

Holy Spirit, I'm guilty of thinking You're here to serve me, a believer. But just as I am, You're here to glorify Jesus Christ. Let my life show that I know this. Amen.

EXPERIENCE *the Power*

FOCUS SCRIPTURE

All of you who were baptized into Christ have clothed yourselves with Christ (Galatians 3:27).

How do your heart, spirit, and life feel different now that you're clothed with Christ and the Power?

_____

_____

_____

FOR REFLECTION

Describe a time you encountered the Holy Spirit as the Power.

_____

_____

_____

Which characteristic of the Power draws you closer to God? Why?

_____

_____

_____

Which message from the devotions this week did you most need—and why?

_____

_____

_____

PERSONAL PRAYER

I praise You, Spirit, as the Power, for…

_____

_____

_____

Forgive me, Spirit, as the Power, when I…

_____

_____

_____

I'm grateful to You, Spirit, as the Power, for…

_____

_____

_____

Spirit, as the Power, today I need Your help to…

_____

_____

_____

When Jesus preached on the kingdom before He left earth, He proclaimed a new standard. He set forth a new way of thinking. He spoke of the rule of God over all, and this rule was to govern believers' lives until His return. It would be different from what the disciples were used to, because God's kingdom is a different realm. The power needed to fully function in this new realm comes from within the realm itself. We have access to the power only through Jesus Christ.

Got to Get Him into Your Life

> When the day of Pentecost had come, they were all together in
> one place. And suddenly there came from heaven a noise like a
> violent rushing wind...And there appeared to them tongues as of
> fire distributing themselves, and they rested on each one of them.

ACTS 2:1-3

Depending on your age, you may be familiar with the song "Got to Get You into My Life" by the band Earth, Wind & Fire. This popular group entered the music scene in the '70s. We're told that when Maurice White, the originator of the group, was naming the band, he looked to astrology. Sagittarius, the sign of the elements, led him to Earth, Wind & Fire. He wanted a name that would let everyone know the band's "electricity" was so strong it could not be ignored. Such was the case during their decades of massive hits.

And such was the case for the Holy Spirit when He showed up while the Israelites were celebrating Pentecost. His appearance and presence were so powerful that He ignited something within these church founders and early members that would not only turn Jerusalem on its heels but go on to engulf the entire globe.

In today's passage we read that the disciples had gathered in one place. And it was in this house and in this moment that the Spirit showed up unexpectedly. It was like a violent, rushing wind had blown through and affected all in its path. What's more, this wind came accompanied by tongues of fire.

The unmistakable presence of God's reality amid God's people transformed the landscape and atmosphere and brought attention to the change taking place such that even those who had gathered from their time of Pentecost were aware of what was happening at this house. It ushered in the beginning of something entirely brand-new: the church.

This is not only an incredible historic event we're talking about. The power of the wind and fire is accessible to us in our lives, circumstances, and experiences right now. But first we have to get Him into our lives.

———

Holy Spirit, I want You in my life. I want the transformation that comes when wind and fire combine to change everything in their path. Change me, Lord. Amen.

Fan the Flame

John answered and said to them all, "As for me, I baptize you with water;
but One is coming who is mightier than I, and I am not fit to untie the
thong of His sandals; He will baptize you with the Holy Spirit and fire."

LUKE 3:16

Why aren't we witnessing the transformative power of the wind and fire today? I believe the Holy Spirit has too often been replaced with sophisticated twenty-first-century formalized Christianity. We celebrate our facilities more than we celebrate the Spirit. We lift up human personalities more than we lift up the Spirit. We have sought to replace Him with entertainment and emotionalism and then wonder why the church isn't on fire. So maybe the better question is this: Why *would* the church be on fire when we have limited the Spirit to our own talents and agendas?

When the Spirit first stormed in, the people of the culture couldn't help but turn their heads and acknowledge that something new, different, and powerful was going on. All around them they witnessed the blaze of the Spirit blowing through, transforming everything it encountered.

But today the world can easily ignore the church when it functions in its own power absent the power of the Spirit. We're living in a time when the Spirit of God has been marginalized. Yes, we hear the Spirit mentioned here or there, but we don't see a rushing wind. We don't see tongues of fire. We don't witness people lit by the presence of God infiltrating the church of God through the manifest presence of the Spirit. Friend, we can have the Acts 2 experience today because we have been baptized with the Holy Spirit and fire. The church is to be the transformational environment for the Spirit of God to affect, infect, and ignite the people of God, resulting in transformed lives that then transfer the values of the kingdom of God to others.

Call on the wind and fire and fan the flame of the Holy Spirit. Let His power transform your heart, home, church, and community.

———

Holy Spirit, I want Your power to consume me and ignite my human spirit. May I live each day seeking Your source of guidance, hope, and transformation. Amen.

New Language of Faith

They were all filled with the Holy Spirit and began to speak with
other tongues, as the Spirit was giving them utterance.

ACTS 2:4

The Holy Spirit gave the disciples the ability to speak human languages they had never learned to speak. The supernatural power took over in such a way that they were able to do what was not natural for them to do on their own. This is how we know it was the Spirit at work and not merely the talents of men.

As a believer, you will also know when the Spirit is working in you, because He will enable you or strengthen you to do what you could never do in your own strength. The Spirit will often give people greater confidence, sharper insight, clearer direction, or even a thought that opens doors for them to serve God in ways they never imagined on their own.

If when I was a child you had told me I would spend my life speaking in front of thousands of people on a regular basis, I would have laughed. After all, I had a persistent stuttering problem. But nothing like that matters to God. The Holy Spirit can overcome and overpower any inadequacy we may face in our physical form.

As believers, many of us aren't experiencing miracles and works of God because we're not full of the Holy Spirit's presence. And because we're not full, we lack His transformative power. Only when we function in His full presence through a committed relationship with Him will we experience the wind and fire setting things aflame in our hearts and in our lives.

The kingdom impact God wants you to make will, more often than not, take you outside of your natural abilities. It will require boldness and trust. It may even require a new language of faith to express the power of the wind and fire in your life.

———

Holy Spirit, replace my words of defeat with words of devotion to Your work in my life. I am ready to be filled with You, Wind and Fire. Amen.

In the Zone

Since we receive a kingdom which cannot be shaken, let us show
gratitude, by which we may offer to God an acceptable service
with reverence and awe; for our God is a consuming fire.

HEBREWS 12:28-29

When baseball players are hitting every pitched ball, people say things like, "They're in the zone." In other words, they're in the flow where everything is clicking and coming together as it should. The Holy Spirit can do the same for you and for me and for our families, churches, and ministries. He wants His kingdom followers to live in the spiritual zone. He wants us in His flow so He can fuel our thoughts and decisions in order to bring Him glory and others good.

Our world is in chaos. Our enemies of the faith are getting bolder than ever before. But we can make a difference when we allow God to fill us with His Spirit so that we're operating in the zone. When we're here, the world will know where we stand. Secularism, socialism, communism, and even capitalism can't mess with God's kingdom and His people when we flow in the power of His Spirit.

God calls this reality being part of His unshakeable kingdom. As Christ's followers, we're part of God's unshakeable kingdom rule—something neither the world nor politics can destroy. This ought to embolden us to live faithful lives under His leading and filled with the wind and fire.

The early church brought God glory because it was burning with the consuming wind and fire of the Holy Spirit. We are to do no less today. People should be seeing what's going on in our lives, homes, churches, and ministries and ask how they can be a part of it. Because when the church and its members are filled with the wind and fire of His Spirit, transformation will sweep over our world. And His works will be known to the glory of His name and the advancement of His kingdom on this earth. Can I get an "Amen"?

———

Holy Spirit, guide my heart so I'm functioning in the zone of Your wonder and miracles. I want Your flame inside of me to be so bright it shows others the way to You. Amen.

EXPERIENCE *the Wind and Fire*

FOCUS SCRIPTURE

Everyone kept feeling a sense of awe; and many wonders and signs were taking place through the apostles (Acts 2:43).

Have you experienced a sense of spiritual awe? What was happening?

_____

_____

_____

FOR REFLECTION

Describe a time you encountered the Holy Spirit as the Wind and Fire.

_____

_____

_____

Which characteristic of the Wind and Fire draws you closer to God? Why?

_____

_____

_____

Which message from the devotions this week did you most need—and why?

_____

_____

_____

PERSONAL PRAYER

I praise You, Spirit, as the Wind and Fire, for…

_____

_____

_____

Forgive me, Spirit, as the Wind and Fire, when I…

_____

_____

_____

I'm grateful to You, Spirit, as the Wind and Fire, for…

_____

_____

_____

Spirit, as the Wind and Fire, today I need Your help to…

_____

_____

_____

Wind and fire were brought down from heaven as the Israelites celebrated the giving of the Ten Commandments to Moses. This was the fiftieth day after the Passover, and they called this celebration Pentecost. Pentecost marked the remembrance of God's deliverance of Israel from Egypt as well as His giving of the Law.